I WILL BE THERE

I will be there

by

MICHAEL HOLLINGS

MOWBRAYS
LONDON & OXFORD
by arrangement with
MAYHEW-McCRIMMON

© *Michael Hollings, 1975*

Text set in Intertype Baskerville
and printed and bound in Great Britain by
Cox & Wyman Ltd, London, Reading and Fakenham

ISBN 0 264 66080 3 *(Mowbrays)*

First published in 1975 by
A. R. Mowbray & Co. Ltd
The Alden Press, Osney Mead, Oxford OX2 OEG

For the people of Southall, Middlesex,
of every colour, class and creed,
among whom I have the joy and struggle of living.
And especially for the parish people
of St Anselm's,
that our growing together
in prayer, love and action
may draw many others to the
love and service of
God and man.

CONTENTS

FOREWORD

This book is a series of meditations or ponderings which take their starting point from some very familiar phrases or titles in St. John's Gospel. These are the titles applied to Jesus which begin: 'I AM . . .'

This is not a text-book but a ponder-book. It is designed to be used either by individuals on their own, or in any form of group. The emphasis is on thought and prayer leading to a deepening in personal and group life. This should then overflow into action both in the local community and in the wider world.

From this, it follows that it is not really suitable for picking up and reading straight through. To do so would be to miss the purpose, and at the same time to risk bringing on a severe attack of indigestion.

The suggested way would be to take it as it is written, slowly, chapter by chapter. If you do this, you will find that within each chapter there is a part where the reader is urged to pause for prayer, reflection or scripture reading as the material demands. The individual should take this as a personal invitation to broadening and deepening. The group may find that discussion will emerge naturally from this area.

Attention to these pauses, and to the themes and questions raised throughout, should help those who wish to do so to make the substance of these meditations real and immediate in their own lives.

It is essentially a practical book, just as prayer is essentially a practical way of life. But both will only be so if you willingly open yourself to the unknown, accepting gladly the repugnance and the lure, the fear and the excitement, the urgency and the boredom, the hate and the love which make up the human reaction to God in Jesus Christ.

I myself am supposed to work in a parish. The pages which follow suffer from the happily frequent interruptions which go with my way of life. That the pages are here at all I owe to the industry of Etta Gullick, without whom the first draft would not have been possible. At later stages I am indebted among others to Madeleine Judd and Anthony Baxter who suggested and corrected and gave a lot of time. Thank you and God bless you all.

In the main I have used excerpts from *The Jerusalem Bible* copyright © 1966 by Darton, Longman & Todd, Ltd. and Doubleday and Company, Inc. by permission from the publisher. Elsewhere I have quoted from the Revised Standard Version of the Bible. I am grateful to the Harvill Press for permission to quote part of a poem by Boris Pasternak from *Dr Zhivago*.

Feast of Corpus Christi 1974   M. H.

I

I AM

Jesus Christ is reported to have said on one occasion:

> Eternal life is this:
> to know you,
> the only true God,
> and Jesus Christ whom you have sent.
>
> *(John 17.3)*

The purpose of the pages which follow is simple. If they contain true reflections on Jesus Christ and what he was showing to the world by his being and his life on earth, then the reader should absorb something more of him. All men, women and children, whether singly or in groups, are within reach of God. But for one reason or another, by no means all seem to be touched by God.

No one will be foolish enough to read this book unless he or she already has at least some interest in God and in Christ, even if this is felt only in a niggling dissatisfaction with life in general, and a sense that there must be 'a lot more to it'.

As one who is happy to be able to affirm that my belief in God and in Christ is very deep, and that it involves a very real experience, I want to make it clear that this belief and experience have not always been as strong and deep as they now are. I say this, because anyone who is going on to read should know that I am quite convinced that we, and therefore our religious attitudes and so on, grow and develop over the years. To be blank now does not mean you will be blank in ten years' time. To believe deeply now does not mean you will necessarily believe in precisely the same way in ten years' time ... indeed, it may well be disastrous if you do! The world and you and I are all evolving. We must not be afraid. I hope we will all go forward in growth; although I do realize that some will fall away from belief rather than advance in it.

I propose, then, to ponder my way through, and I ask you to ponder with me, either while studying the text itself, or in silent thinking out and growth as a development from the text. Look at Jesus, think about him, stay with him, question him, listen to him, discuss him. I want his Spirit to lead us, and I want us to be conscious that it is only his Spirit which is any good as a guide. I want us to be aware that his Spirit will guide us so that we can share in that living love and love of living which will allow the realization in ourselves of Paul's prayer for the Ephesians:

> Out of his infinite glory, may he give you the power through his Spirit for your hidden self to grow strong, so that Christ may live in your hearts through faith, and then, planted in love and built on love, you will with all the saints have strength to grasp the breadth and the length, the height and the depth; until, knowing the love of Christ, which is beyond all knowledge, you are filled with the utter fullness of God. (*Eph. 3.16–19*)

But, in order to ponder, we must begin with silence.

I want you to start now in a practical way by stopping your reading. I want you to take the chapter heading. Then sit still, quiet and empty, without trying to *think*, indeed in a way trying not to think. I want you to hold Christ's words: 'I AM ...' Just hold them ... now ... for two full minutes ... now!

I am thoroughly in earnest about this silence. If you dismissed my request, and so skipped the experiencing of the silence just now, will you please go back and really do what I asked ... 'Pause a while and know that I am God ...'

Now, to continue!

The Old Testament gives us accounts of conversations with God. Why? Well, humanly it is very difficult to express communication without using some humanly recognizable form. If something is to be communicated, we can achieve this by a sign that can be seen, a gesture for instance. We can achieve it by touch, as when one stretches out one's hand to restrain a friend who is unwittingly about to disturb children engaged in a secret game. Or again, and most commonly, we can communicate by word of mouth. It is natural, then, that we should think and talk of God speaking to man. In doing so, however, we run the risk of losing sight of the brilliant truth which Ivan Illych points out in his *Celebration of Awareness*: 'Only the Christian believes in the Word as co-eternal Silence.'

Perhaps it is fanciful of me, but I understand the times Moses spent with God as times of thunder and times of deep silence. Out of the silence, God spoke in silence. He opened the mind and heart of the prophet not by stringing together the human sounds and ideas which we use to communicate, often so superficially. Rather he en-silenced the being of Moses. And in this way, Moses came to know what was beyond knowing and beyond words. Then there arose for Moses the problem: he was baffled as to how he could communicate to God's people, in a way they would understand, the mystery God had spoken to him by silence. When he questioned God on this, God said to him: 'I Am who I Am ... This is what you must say to the sons of Israel: "I Am has sent me to you".' (*Exod. 3.14*)

Our danger is that since then the message given out of silence has been passed on in multitudes of words. Instead of being en-silenced, we have become wordy.

Of course, as human beings we need words, gestures,

pictures, sounds, and all these aids . . . but we also need silence.

How difficult it is to teach people to be silent. Because so much emphasis is put on communicating, the communication of silence is neglected or not understood. We must learn the sensitivity of silence: listening to silence, open to the sound of silence, bathed in the peace of silence, skilled to pick up the length of silence, its weight and lightness. Some may be naturally silent and may readily appreciate silence and enjoy it; others are awkward and nervous in any prolonged silence; they shift and cough, and itch to start speaking. Yet all, to my mind, need to cultivate true silence which is deep, reflective, open and receptive, developing . . . real.

We are told that at a certain point Jesus, seemingly echoing this conversation between Moses and God, applied to himself the words: I AM. (*John 8.58*). Interestingly the text which includes this passage remarks that Jesus was speaking 'to the Jews who believed in him'. But what he said in human words was too much for them to accept. Gradually wrath and condemnation grew in them, possibly together with misunderstanding, until they ended by picking up stones to throw at him.

I find this very significant: what he said was too much for them to take. But had they been willing to sit down with Jesus, to ponder and discuss the underlying meaning of what he said and claimed, they might well have come round, after doubt, to say with Thomas, 'My Lord and my God'.

In the fourth Gospel, which we call the Gospel according to St. John, there are a series of statements about Jesus each starting with I AM, and throughout this book, chapter by chapter, we shall look at these 'I AMs' in turn. We must remember that these titles applied by his disciples to Jesus give us a distilled vision of him. They are reflections yielding true insight, and are very natural to the more contemplative style of writing. Each one can help us to know the only true God and Jesus Christ whom he has sent, if we set ourselves ready and open to learn. The present chapter is somewhat different, in that here the I AM stands by itself, and is at its most basic, most central, and least understandable.

I AM ... the whole of our belief in God which continually deepens and turns to knowledge is summed up there ... I AM. Ceaseless reasoning of philosophers and debate of theologians culminates there. It is comprehensive in its simplicity. If you have (or can make) the time, sit down every day with that phrase on your mind and in your heart, until it is absorbed into your whole being. Then you can live and move in the acceptance of the wonder and beauty, the immensity and life of the One who has the power and simplicity to state himself silently as I AM.

It is not easy in the busy-ness of our lives to still ourselves. Silence makes us uneasy; it is too immeasurably big to be comfortable. It beats on us; we want to shift and talk, to use our minds on problems they can tackle. But if we run from silence to noise we are running from the deeper to the shallower; from the silence of God to the noise of the world. Even when we meet his Word, spoken in Jesus Christ, he is characteristically silent. He lives quietly in obscurity for most of his life. Later he spoke, but did not write; his message was carried on from mouth to mouth and from heart to heart, deeply pondered before bearing fruit.

Among the ponderings come down to us the 'I AMs'. And the last – and I hope lasting – consideration at this point is this. Think of 'I AM' as meaning 'I WILL BE THERE'. No matter where you turn, Jesus will be there; no matter what emptiness you feel, Jesus will be there; when you are in most wretched pain in mind or body, Jesus will be there; when you are filled with unutterable love and joy, Jesus will be there; when you are lost, Jesus will be there; when you move through life ordinarily and plainly, without much excitement or much to say, Jesus

13

will be there; when you are silent in prayer, Jesus will be there; and finally when you die, Jesus will be there, and you will know forever what it means when he says, 'I AM'.

2

I AM THE WAY

J. R. R. Tolkien, in his masterpiece *The Lord of the Rings*, has a beautiful passage in which the Council of Elrond is sitting to decide who shall take the Ring. It is difficult. Old Bilbo gets impatient:

'Can't you think of some names now? Or put it off till after dinner?'
No one answered. The noon-bell rang. Still no one spoke. Frodo glanced at all the faces, but they were not turned to him. All the Council sat with downcast eyes, as if in deep thought. A great dread fell on him, as if he was awaiting the pronouncement of some doom he had long foreseen and vainly hoped might after all never be spoken. An overwhelming longing to rest and remain at peace by Bilbo's side in Rivendell filled all his heart. At last with an effort he spoke, and wondered to hear his own words, as if some other will was using his small voice.
'I will take the Ring,' he said, 'though I do not know the way.'

I have personally often felt that kind of pull, in greater or lesser degree, but perhaps never more than on the two occasions when God seemed to be 'getting at me'. The first was when I had to decide to say once more after a period of disbelief that I believed in God, with all the vastness of commitment that that might mean. The second was when I felt my life had to be led in the or-dained priesthood, with the necessary giving up of a career, in my case the giving up of marriage and family, and the dark outreach of a way given to unselfish service of others. On both occasions, there was a personal understanding of Frodo's feelings.

You will almost certainly have had similar experiences at one time or another. They are not necessarily very dramatic. They are expressed by Paul writing to the Galatians: 'The desires of the flesh are against the Spirit, and the desires of the Spirit are against the flesh; for these are opposed to each other, to prevent you from doing what you would.' (Gal. 5. 17) This does not refer simply to sexual indulgence, but to any self-indulgence. For instance, it is so often easy to put off the evil moment of beginning something which we know we should do, whether it is getting up in the morning, writing a letter or kneeling down to pray. Quite frequently, we tell ourselves that we do not know the way to tackle a situation, the words to use in a letter. Another excuse we use, particularly in regard to making time to pray, is that life is too busy. And so we dither and dally and find a hundred and one things to be done – and do not pray.

But so far as God is concerned, we would do well to stop a moment and think of his Eternity. The words the Psalmist addresses to God may at present mean little to us:

To you, a thousand years are a single day,
a yesterday now over, an hour of the night.
(*Ps. 90*)

This is the reality of the matter, however, and we need to cultivate in our own lives that contact with the Eternal which will give depth and balance to our being.

In trying to do so, it may help to think how even to us time can seem to vary its length in our lives. Do you ever remember waiting for a train which seemed as though it would never come? Or yearning for the end of a pain-filled night? Did you ever try to linger over the last sad moments of a parting, or put off the time when you had to go back to school? On all occasions of such a kind we try either to speed up or slow down the passing of time; and it does seem to us as though some moments last for ever and others are gone in a flash.

I mentioned earlier the idea of the Word as 'co-eternal Silence'. To experience prayer is to begin to know something of both this eternity and this silence.

Physically, there are various ways of 'stilling' oneself, methods well tried and much used: special ways of sitting, deep and slow breathing, saying a simple word or phrase in repetition . . . and so on.

Mentally, it is important to 'accept' the eternity and the silence of God if we are to grow in this way of stillness. By this I mean that whether we sit, kneel or stand, we must be in an attitude of faith, open, 'unknowing'. We cannot really understand, because eternity is beyond the understanding of our finite minds. However, we can accept and 'hold' the sense of eternity in stillness. If we do so – something happens.

It is like going to sleep at night with something unresolved on the mind, and waking up the following morning to find the solution very clear. Sleep is one of the silences, when our inner self, our subconscious, has greater freedom, because we have stopped piling it with accumulated data. (Among students this seems to happen very noticeably, for example, with those doing mathematics.) Problems which appear to have no solution when the mind is willed to be working on them, as it were work themselves out when the mind is free-wheeling, or even working in another field. Somehow, the solution slips in underneath consciousness, and rises out of the quietness of mind.

If you do not know it to be true from your own experience, please accept this sort of thing does happen in prayer. Though not understanding how, accept that it can happen to you. And then go on to accept that God speaks to us out of his eternity in the silences of our lives, and especially through prayer. Pause a moment to make such a silence in your life . . .

Let us now consider the way in which Jesus, the Eternal Word, presented himself to his disciples. He very often used parables. He did not make himself clear; he did not spell out directly what he was trying to teach, but led them obliquely, through telling them a story, to draw a deep meaning and lesson.

With this in mind we can see the whole of life as a parable, for we can be learning constantly by watching the world and people. We may not seem to be relating directly to God, yet since we believe in God as creator, we can say that anything and everything speaks to us of him in some way, if we are open and have ears to hear and eyes to see.

As Gerard Manley Hopkins wrote:

Why do men then now not reck his rod?
Generations have trod, have trod, have trod;
  And all is seared with trade; bleared, smeared with toil;
  And wears man's smudge and shares man's smell: the soil
Is bare now, nor can foot feel, being shod.

So much is learnt about God and his workings indirectly. To absorb the lessons of the world we have to be patient, reading the signs of the times, learning of men and women. We must look at nature, the failures of nature as well as its beauties ... So that through the whole parable we realize more deeply the grandeur of God.

This is all part of finding the way, though to the tidy-minded it may seem a long way round! It is dangerous to think that it is easy to know and love God directly, as John points out in his first letter:

A man who does not love the brother that he can see cannot love God, whom he has never seen.

(*1 John 4.20*)

There is very much more in the phrase 'seeing Christ in

each person you meet' than is apparent from the ease with which it can be said. If I meet you, I do not *exactly* meet Christ, even though you are 'en-Christed'. And indeed, depending on the mingling in you of humanity and godliness (or the lack of both!) I can either be led to recognize Christ ... or I can actually have his image obscured by you! If then we can approach people and the world as a constant source of further knowledge, both of good and of evil, there is hope that we shall at all times be ready to learn, whether from beauty, joy, friendship, love – or (by the reverse process) in reaction to hate, ugliness, sorrow, unfriendliness.

Then again, we can come to learn about Jesus Christ as a man. When we meet another man, though he may not show us Christ directly, there is the amazing fact that we can look at that man and say: 'How extraordinary! Jesus Christ was a man! If I had lived when he did, I could have come round the corner and met him face to face. He really was once a little child, really played in the streets of Nazareth, really ate and slept!' In this way another man encountered in the street or wherever can speak a parable to us of Jesus and of God.

We may still however tend to complain that we do not sufficiently know the way to set about meeting Christ in things and in people. If this is a problem to us, then we could usefully look to see how Jesus Christ set about meeting *us*! He did it in a human way, and he led his disciples through to knowledge in a human way. He was with them, and he grew alongside them 'in wisdom and grace before God and man'. Sometimes people get worried and confused that Christ never wrote anything down, but allowed everything to come through by word of mouth. I personally find this encouraging and entirely in keeping with the sensitive approach of God to man.

Growth is a dimension of which we do well to remind ourselves at this point as we study Jesus, try to find our way to him, and confront him reportedly claiming to be 'the Way'. Jesus himself grew; and he lived with his disciples and allowed them to grow in discovering him. This they did gradually, hesitantly. They went in a see-saw from overwhelming sense of his power (Peter's 'depart from me, for I am a sinful man') to the very human reaction of fear of ridicule for associating with him (Peter again: 'I know not the man').

What we have handed down to us by word of mouth and by the writings of the New Testament is the distilled knowledge of Jesus Christ, clarified and brought to fullness by the Spirit in the living life of his followers. We cannot, I suppose, be certain that Jesus ever said precisely: 'I am the way'. In the course of being with those he knew and taught, he may well indeed have uttered this phrase in so many words. But it does not really matter whether he did or not. The truth which is important to us is that all he is, all he teaches, the discipleship he requires, can be summed up by putting into his mouth at a later date the clear statement:

'I AM THE WAY.' (*John 14.6*)

What can his disciples mean in telling us that he says this of himself? They cannot mean that he literally wants us to walk on him. We cannot lay him down like a red carpet, a primrose path, or even a way of the cross.

Anyone can understand how an ordinary human being can lead the way. He can do this by word and example, and by going out ahead as a person. The prophets and teachers of the Old Testament did just this, sometimes against their will, always somehow driven or led into the role by God. They pleaded they were children, they did not know how to speak, and so on: but the power of God and the spirit of his message showed each of them a path forward, and opened or re-opened the way to the children of Israel. Then eventually, through John the Baptist, the message rang louder and clearer than at any previous time.

I am, as Isaiah prophesied:
'a voice that cries in the wilderness:
Make a straight way for the Lord'. (*John 1.23*)

But still he is only a voice. He makes no claim to be the way. He is the 'pathfinder'.

For Jesus the claim is direct. 'I AM THE WAY.' In ascribing this to him his followers put forward something fundamentally different from anything which had been said before in the history of prophecy in the Jewish tradition. This claim is supported by John the Baptist who points to the Way, and directs his own followers from himself straight to Jesus: 'Look, there is the Lamb of God.' (*John 1.36*)

Jesus is not one who points out the way, except in so far as he points at himself. He calls on men, who are made in the image of God, to be godly: 'You must therefore be perfect just as your heavenly Father is perfect' (*Matt. 5.48*), or 'Learn of me because I am gentle and humble in heart' (*Matt. 11.29*).

He can say with complete simplicity, authority and truth: 'I am the way', but this immediately puts us in a difficulty which is well summed up by G. K. Chesterton:

The way is all so very straight
That we may lose the way.

The basic and 'unbelievable' fact is that the Way is Jesus Christ, who is God and man. As we move further and further from the time of Christ, we may, to be sure, get bogged down in problems of philosophy and theology when it comes to expressing this reality in the appropriate language. Indeed, we may almost fear to say anything at all, in case we formulate the reality in the wrong way. But the deep and central truth, whose sense all words are inadequate to convey, is that in Jesus Christ we have God-man. It is our very efforts to clarify this truth in ideas and words that tend to distract us from its simple straightness.

If we can 'see', then in wonder we understand that he is the expression for all men to see of God-in-the-world. He is saying in and through his life: If you want to understand how God works in the human being – look at me. If you want to know what God expects from the human being – look at me. If you want to know how God would react in human nature in a human situation which is real – look at me.

There never has been, and there never will be (so far as we know), another man of whom this can be said, because Jesus alone is God-man.

Now if anyone says to another person: 'In this situation you would react in such and such a way', the latter can reply: 'How do you know? You are not me, and I am the only one who knows how I will react.' The first person may well rejoin that he has known the other for a long time, and probably understands his character better than he understands it himself. But the fact remains that the human individual is not wholly predictable. The subject here is still himself, and in reality neither person can be completely sure how he will react in the future.

The problem of man in relation to God is that man does go in for predicting God's reaction, and doing it dogmatically – and quite often getting it wrong! The jolt supplied by Jesus Christ was that he came along and said with authority: 'You say ... but I say ...!' In the years when Jesus lived, man's interpretation of God's word was at variance with the reality, as it was lived by God's Word-made-flesh in Christ.

It would be a good thing at this point to stop and ponder. For each of us is I believe to some degree guilty of this misplaced assumption of knowledge about God and his 'attitude' to the events of life in the world. Let us take the passage immediately before Christ's statement that he is 'the Way, the Truth and the Life'. It is in John 14.4–5. Jesus says: 'You know the way to the place where I am going.' Thomas comments: 'Lord, we do not know where you are going, so how can we know the way?'

At that place and time, Thomas had no grasp of what Christ was talking about, and so he comes out with the very straight and simple conclusion that because they do not know where Jesus is going, they do not know the way to it. But this is the point at which to stop. The straight, simple, very human conclusion is so lacking in real insight that it cannot even begin to imagine the vision which comes to hit it: I AM THE WAY.

So, pause and wait on the thought that all our ideas and imaginings may fall as far short of the reality of Jesus Christ as Thomas's question falls short of Jesus' reply! And of course, even the statement: 'I am the way' is inadequate: which gives all the more reason for stopping and emptying our minds, so that he may fill them in his own way, which is beyond our unaided human understanding.

Perhaps now we can begin to feel how 'Jesus the Way' can make sense. It is no road, but a person. It is not merely the following of a person, though this following goes without saying through the whole idea. No, it is being so closely united to the person – Jesus Christ – that the person, the follower, the following and the way are united.

Here again, it is possible to get into trouble with words! If I say all these merge, I can be charged with pantheism. But I would none the less hazard the expression that the follower follows so closely he 'becomes' the way because, following Jesus, he is where Jesus is; being on the way and in the way (Jesus being the way) he is united to the way as though his feet have become immovably fastened to a moving staircase. What is more, it is as though the rhythm of the staircase has entered his brain and now beats in his heartbeat and is breathed in his breathing.

This is one reason why the development of prayer life as an essential element in following the way flows more easily with some regularity and rhythm. An example of this is the effectiveness of such a 'system' as the Jesus Prayer. Take the words: 'Lord Jesus Christ, Son of God, have mercy on me', pattern them to your breathing

. . . Lord Jesus Christ, Son of God, have mercy on me . . .
Lord Jesus Christ, Son of God, have mercy on me
. . . Lord Jesus Christ, Son of God, have mercy on me.
Draw this out, taste it, breathe it, until it, the rhythm and
your very self all seem to merge . . . and let this grow from
a series of forced acts into a habit. As you go on, you will
find there is real rhythm. You will sense the prayer as full
of godliness. You will become seized by it, and it will continue almost unconsciously throughout not only your
waking but even part of your sleeping.

The early monk, Cassian, wrote to the effect that the
monk is not praying until he does not know he is praying.

The distinctive thing here is that although being on the
way and united to the way becomes an unconscious reality, at the same time, because the way is a person, the
reality takes on the language of love. I really am 'wedded'
to Jesus who is the way. Subconsciously, I am always
basically aware of this committed relationship. This
brings with it a deepening joy of realization, a tranquillity, radiance and thanksgiving.

A close analogy can be seen in the case of the rich
young man who came to Jesus. He asked what he had to
do for eternal life, and Jesus answered equally simply:
'Keep the commandments.' The young man felt he had
done that all his life, and yet he was still not satisfied. So
Jesus, looking at him and loving him, gives him the challenge which is *the* challenge: 'Sell all you have and come
and follow me.' . . . 'Get going, get on the way, get one
with the way, be wholly given to the way in living and
loving.' In the context this whole command is like the
Genesis words of the Creator echoed by Christ in answering the Pharisees: 'This is why a man must leave father
and mother, and cling to his wife, and the two become
one body. They are no longer two, therefore, but one
body.' (*Matt. 19.5–6*).

Such a phrase is devastating in its straight simplicity. It
faces us with a basic difficulty . . . it is hard for us to take

24

Jesus Christ at his word. It is difficult to accept he means it, when he says: 'Leave all and follow me'; it is especially difficult to think he could mean *me*! It is difficult to accept he means it when he says: 'Your sins are forgiven', or 'I will make *you* fishers of men', or 'Fear not; I have overcome the world'; or: 'Take up your cross daily and follow me'.

Precisely because it is very simple, we fail to understand. It may help to look at things as follows. God's original instruction, we are told in the Old Testament, was not to eat of the tree of the knowledge of good and evil (whatever exactly that means). With disobedience following this command, God gave another simple one: 'Go out and increase and multiply and subdue the earth.' Again a simple instruction ... but very difficult to do, apparently.

What happened? Simplicity tended to grow into complexity because of the familiar reaction of human beings to rules and laws. We are inclined to seek clarification of method. If the commandment is 'Love God', the human being says, *'How* should I love God?'. If the commandment is 'Love your neighbour', the human being says, *'How* do I love my neighbour?'. And so two simple commandments are explained and amplified into ten ... Moreover, the human being then wants to know Who exactly *is* 'my neighbour'? And this in turn leads to further explanation and definition ...

Instead of being silent, and open, instead of listening to God in their hearts, people seek human reassurance, written or spoken, to form a measure for their conduct. The simple, straight command: 'Love God, love your neighbour' becomes a labyrinth of different ways, cul-de-sacs, blind alleys, roundabouts – with the priests and the doctors of the law acting as policemen!

When John the Baptist came, he had to cut through the mountains of regulations, bulldoze legalism. He had to simplify the code of behaviour which had led to confusion of mind and the misplacing of values. In his day (as in ours) there were different readings of the same scripture passage, different interpretations of the Law. There was that familiar problem of the same society breeding at the same time scrupulousness and unscrupulousness! There were 'religious' people who were indifferent; and equally 'religious' who were zealots. There had to be with John a great levelling – but a levelling *up* not a levelling *down*. (Today's society and today's reconcilers should be clear about this!)

The approach of the Baptist was radical – back to simplicity; away with hypocrisy! The levelling and the straightness were for one purpose only – preparing the way of the Lord ... so that the Lord could provide a straight path to the Father ... a straight path which was himself.

At the time of Christ, as is still true today, there were many different people claiming to be prophets and teachers. The people of Israel was supposedly one people. But within it there were tribes and also different parties ... Sadducees, Pharisees, Scribes and so on. Between them they managed both to reach the heights, and also to reduce the wonder and beauty of God's revelation to an imprisoning code of law. John cut across this with a simple call to repentance.

There was nothing profoundly new in John. He was not 'The Way', but he emphasized dependence on God in faith, as against over-emphasis on the Law. He introduced a breathing space to re-introduce the silence of the desert. He was spring-cleaning, setting God's house in order, because 'The Way' when he came was to fall foul of people who were over-cluttered by busy-ness, rules, practices, the care of many things. This was one reason why the Word, The Way: 'Came to his own domain, and his own people did not accept him.' (*John 1.11*)

Few of us like to be shaken out of 'our way'. Few immediately respond well to being told to wake their ideas up, and discard treasured habits of mind and action. Few have the humility and faith to accept the possibility of being on the wrong way or just at a standstill and needing to move on.

The message of Jesus, developing the opening barrage of John the Baptist, is essentially uncomfortable and can be disruptive of personal and society living.

But unless there is simplicity, and out of simplicity silence, we get overgrown and need cutting and pruning. The simplicity of Jesus is like some modern discoveries. It cuts through like a laser beam; its impact is as quick as 'subliminal' advertising, when something is flashed on a screen too quickly for us consciously to 'see' it, yet it penetrates our subconscious minds. Thus with Jesus. You do not immediately have to understand, but you have to listen. You cannot necessarily 'feel' his presence, but he penetrates. Later you may say 'I know', without knowing how you know. You may later act differently, hardly knowing why.

Jesus is that sort of person.

He is completely simple and single with God, because he is God. His whole being is well beyond anything my wonderful but finite mind can comprehend. It is a funny thing really! We are meant to go on learning about God, and people will tell us to study this, read that – but the things you and I actually learn with our minds are relatively shallow. It is as though we behaved with ordinary people by getting to know them simply by looking, and not also by listening, talking and so on. We need to accept with Jesus that there is deeper communication than thinking.

He expressed this in his own life by being about with his disciples, and himself 'being about with God', and marrying the two aspects into one whole way . . . Himself. He wants us to know that by ourselves, even with intense mental effort, we cannot come far in the knowledge of God. But his method of working is through the openness of our minds, through silence and that mysterious thing called faith. Given those conditions, which we can cultivate with his aid, he penetrates deeply and infiltrates 'knowledge beyond knowledge'.

This 'unknowing knowledge' is the depth of his way, and to use another analogy it penetrates us rather as heat does when it is communicated by closeness, body-warmth. We become radiated by Christ if we hug so close to him that we share his light and life. As with deep-ray treatment, we do not immediately feel the warmth, and perhaps oddly it is often other people who notice the change in us before we do ourselves.

This cannot really be put into words. Only by reacting openly to God's plan, resting in silence, accepting God's way of working in us will the truth penetrate. So what am I trying to say? I am trying to express what I think Jesus was stressing when his followers understood him as 'the Way, the Truth and the Life'. He made it as clear as possible to those with ears and eyes that because he is the way, we must go along with him. But this 'along' is through him, with him and in him.

We go through him, and later we study this in his revolation: 'I am the door.' We go with him, because he is life, and we are baptised into his Body and live from his flesh which is life indeed. This is God's Way, and God's Way is Jesus Christ.

The meaning is as plain and as obscure as Jesus Christ himself. And so it takes us back to the quotation from J. R. R. Tolkien, and Frodo. If you feel at once like echoing Frodo and saying 'Yes' to God's call, yet also insisting with him: '. . . but I do not know the way' . . . then sit quietly and ponder the Gospel words of Jesus:

'I AM THE WAY.'

3

I AM THE DOOR

At first glance, the idea of Christ as 'the Door' was not one which inspired me in my reading of Scripture or in my prayer life. What about you? I confess to a recurrent and childish distraction, a conundrum posed in school days – When is a door not a door? The answer was not 'When it is Jesus Christ'. That it was not shows how slow we are to exploit ideas and phrases which at first seem empty. Christ himself was wonderful at parables. It is a pity we are not better geared to surprise each other with the kind of 'mind-jerker' which must often have been there when Jesus made his points.

Will you please read through the passage with which we are now concerned? Do you know where it comes? Do you remember what came immediately before and what followed? ... Do get your Bible now and read it (*John chapter 10*), otherwise you will not follow what I am going to say.

Have you done that? Because if you have not, what I say will mean nothing ... and please do not say 'I know the place' without first getting that Bible, finding the passage, and having the humility to read it ...

One interesting thing about our passage in the Gospel is the setting. Immediately before is the story of the man born blind and cured by Jesus. And right after our passage the listeners return to this extraordinary and wonderful event in the life of this very ordinary man. He was born blind. Suddenly Jesus came into his life – and he could see. Unable to deny that his blindness was cured, the Jews continued to find different explanations for

Jesus' power. Some asserted he was possessed and raving; others questioned this. Could a devil open the eyes of the blind?

In the middle come the two powerful images of Jesus Christ: the Door or Gate, and the Shepherd.

Now Christ spoke to a local people, a shepherd people, all of whom would understand his figures of speech as well as you would if I today were to refer to astronauts, count-downs and so on. He was referring to the entrance to the sheepfold and the shepherd. You may already know this or not, depending on how much you have read: in the Israel of Jesus' day the sheepfold was normally a barrier of stones, with only one point of entry. The sheep were led or driven in. But there was no 'door' or 'gate' as such. Danger came at night, and then the shepherd secured the gap of the opening to the enclosure either by his vigilance or by his very body. Sheep-stealing was not done on a glamorous Hollywood technicolor basis, but through some silent, stealthy, nocturnal entry into the sheepfold by some way other than the gap or door.

In spite of appreciating the setting and hearing Christ's initial exposition, the Jews we are told did not understand what he was getting at (or perhaps pretended not to, because it was too pointed!). See John 10.1–6. So Jesus went on quite explicitly: 'I am the door of the sheepfold.'

Given that this is the immediate teaching that the writer wants his readers to learn, we must look at it ourselves. But there is a question raised by this idea, a question we cannot hope to discuss fully, but one we must at least touch on. It is this . . . Jesus is shepherd and door – is it true that no one can be saved except through him?

In another passage of John's Gospel Jesus says: 'No one can come to the Father except through me.'

Now, there are those Christians who interpret the Scriptures by not interpreting them . . . that is they take them completely literally. If you do this you are left with a seemingly narrow gate and straight way, and salvation for relatively few, those who *consciously* are followers of

Christ. *This* is the only way to the Father, that is to say to 'eternal life'.

Such literal interpretation has led to centuries of crying out 'No salvation outside the church', with this often understood in a very rigid way. But today we are living in a world which from one angle is called 'developing' and from another 'shrinking'. As a result, our assessment of foreign peoples and cultures has had to be revised. We must regard all men as our equals ... not really a very popular idea, and not very well lived out! Racial and religious tolerance and intolerance have to some extent tended to go along together, though involving very different principles. But the interesting thing for Christians in the West, anyhow, is that we are not only faced by the spread of indifference to religion among perhaps the majority of people, but also by the devoted living out of religion by many upon many who do not give Christ a central position in belief or worship, or do not even admit him at all.

My plea here, before going on to the Christian encounter with Christ as door, is that all Christians try to shed their ignorance and fear of non-Christian religions, and begin to open their eyes and minds to the wealth, beauty and spirituality of the huge treasury of Eastern writings, Jewish writings and so on. Many Christians, in my limited experience have not sat down to consider Judaism and 'pagan religions' in prayer and a spirit of interest and learning.

It would be completely beyond me and the outside the competence of this small book to tackle the profound problems of theology involved between Christians and non-Christians. I just want to indicate what I believe to be a very positive attitude which we can cultivate. For instance, what a huge amount we have in common with the Jews, how much common literature in the Bible, how much common prayer in the Psalms. And what about this evening prayer taken from the Authorized Daily Prayer Book:

Blessed be the Lord by day; blessed be the Lord by night; blessed be the Lord when we lie down; blessed be the Lord when we rise up. For in thy hands are the souls of the living and the dead, as it is said. In his hand is the soul of every living thing, and the spirit of all human flesh. Into thy hands I commend my spirit; thou hast redeemed me, O Lord God of truth. Our God who art in heaven, assert the unity of thy name, and establish thy kingdom continually, and reign over us for ever and ever.

We who worship the God of Abraham, Isaac and Jacob with the Jews can surely share spiritually with them, and rejoice at our common heritage in the one true God!

It is different in regard to, say, the followers of Mohammed, though they both believe in the one God and also count Jesus as a prophet. But here again, their worship is full of prayer and praise, which is not contradictory to what we should wish to express. The use of such prayer can, in my opinion help us to closer racial and cultural relationship, to say nothing of religious understanding, while not abandoning anything of our own worship of God, Father, Son and Holy Spirit. Take this for instance:

Praise be to him who when I call on him answers me, slow though I am when he calls me.

Praise be to him who gives to me when I ask him, miserly though I am when he asks a loan of me.

Praise be to him to whom I confide my needs whensoever I will and he satisfies them.

My Lord I praise thee, for thou art of my praise most worthy.

In my own personal life at the moment of writing, I am living in a high concentration area of the Sikh community, and so in the past four years I have done what I could in a small way to study the life and teaching of Guru Nanak and the other Gurus. Once more, there is a real mine of beauty and spiritual expression in their writings and prayers. Here is a Sikh example to add to the others:

> There is one God,
> He is the Supreme Truth,
> He, the Creator, is without fear
> And without hate.
> He, the Omnipresent, pervades the Universe.
> He is not born, nor does he die to be born again.
> True in the beginning, true throughout the ages,
> True even now, and forever shall be true.

There is still the problem of Jesus as the door. I as a Christian accept him as the way into all truth, but I am left with the consciousness of the extent of truth taught, practised and lived by those who, while in their own way believing devoutly in God, do not accept Christ as the door. When I see him, and see their goodness and insight, I am perplexed. Should not anyone with such qualities understand Jesus?

Here we face the immense and beautiful variety of human nature, which is so varied that some of the variations we understand and like, some we accept and tolerate, and some we simply cannot fathom and instinctively abhor. But God is over all, made all, loves all.

Then of course the further question arises: How exactly can I grasp God's 'reaction' to an agnostic or again to an 'atheist', a person who is urgent for good, who strives for the truth, and who remains uncommitted or even theoretically opposed? How can I view a person who seems to accept so much of what I do, yet at a certain point stops short, and begins to argue or find excuses? Is this malice, laziness, stupidity, fear? Or does God have some purpose for them which I perhaps cannot see, but which is within the vastness of his plan?

For me there is the belief that Christ is God, Redeemer, Lord and Brother. Through him I come to the Father.

But personally I find it easy to believe also that he is the Lord of these others as well, the countless millions who have never properly heard of him, or who ignore, reject, intellectualize, scorn, long-for, seek, hate, love-in-a-mist, and so on. I have no idea how he works it out, this great God in whom I trust. But I know he came for all men, and I am happy that somehow beyond anything I grasp is the possibility of their being involved in his saving pattern and moving through the door, provided they are not kept separate by malice.

It is fortunate, perhaps, that this kind of thing cannot be fully understood. We do not know everything. There are mysteries. Once more, for me, the way forward and through the Door which deepens perception is by prayer, contemplation, and an enlightenment God sends beyond the reason.

So with that, let us turn as Christians to Jesus, the Door. How similar is the idea to that of 'the way'! But it is a very modern idea as well as being ancient, and it indicates entry to a whole new world of experience, indeed to a new dimension. And what is spelt out for us by Jesus is that he has come for the purpose of making entry to this new dimension possible for ordinary human beings. A homely illustration is in *Alice Through the Looking Glass*, where Alice comes up against the glass and it turns into a sort of mist, and then she is through. Once there: 'She began looking about, and noticed that what could be seen from the old room was quite common and uninteresting, but that all the rest was as different as possible. For instance, the pictures on the wall next to the fire seemed to be alive, and the very clock on the chimney-piece (you know you can only see the back of it in the Looking-glass) had got the face of a little old man, and grinned at her.' Everything is back to front, everything is new, and there is a certain parallel between the Looking-glass world and the world of Jesus Christ, because so often the things of Jesus Christ seem all back-to-front in our ordinary world, but they are alive!

Look at the examples: The Lord says you have got to be weak to be strong; the Lord says the meek will inherit the earth, while the world says this is not true at all, for you must be strong and powerful. The Lord says unless you die, you will not live; the world says protect your life at all costs. The Lord says in order to be rich, you must give away all you have. The Lord says he who is the master comes as the servant of all. The Lord says the last will be first and the first last . . . looking-glass notions!

And so it is not surprising that this demand of Jesus is also a bit back to front . . . Go through a person who is a door, and do this as an act of faith, not really knowing what is on the other side! This is why the image of death is important, because you have to step out into a door which does not seem to be there, trusting that it is open, you have to go through it, leaving everything behind . . . you may well come to feel like the apostles . . . We have left everything to follow you! What do we get out of it?

If we pause to think of these commands and demands, we may understand more clearly how completely we have to give. There is a passage in C. S. Lewis' *The Last Battle* which sums up the difficulty this decision to go through may cause in us: The Lion is talking:

'You see,' said Aslan, 'they will not let us help them. They have chosen cunning instead of belief. Their prison is only in their own minds, yet they are in that prison; and so afraid of being taken in that they cannot be taken out. But come, children, I have other work to do.'

He went to the Door and they all followed him.

In a certain sense, a door cannot give itself more than by being open; in a certain sense this is exactly what Christ does: he says here I am; I am completely humble, completely open, completely given for you . . . I am the door. All you have to do is make the step through in faith. But to do so, you yourself will need to be completely humble, completely open, completely given in full faith and trust.

He says this, because he has told us elsewhere that the gate is narrow and the way is straight, and if we are cluttered up with all the baggage of our self-conceit, all the trappings of our worldly goods, all the bristles and angles of our insecurity and distrust – then we shall get stuck in the door and never get through. The solution is just to strip all this off; shake yourself. Rather like a process of slimming, you will fit where you did not fit before!

These are only analogies, but they reflect the looking-glass world, which is further turned inside out by the fact that as we look round at ourselves and the Church, clergy, religious and laity alike, we seem firmly stuck the *home* side of the looking-glass. Everything is very much the right way round from this world's standpoint with wealth, position, drive to the top, and all the other things Christ's looking-glass world reverses.

Humanly it is so much safer to say to myself I have my little bit, I am going to shut myself in, keep safe and not venture very far. This is easier than saying: Here you are, Lord, take the lot! . . . by which process we suddenly discover we are through the door.

The thing with Alice was that when she was once through she was through, but she nevertheless had to go on and on experiencing the differences. There is even a sense for us in which living in Christ is a combination of reality and dreamworld, only the dreamworld points up and clarifies the reality. In this we ourselves experience ever more deeply the sense of being utterly dependent upon God. And yet sometimes 'God is not there' . . . and how can one bear to be dependent upon someone who is not there?

Well the fact is that here again our human values are up-ended by being through the door. So we may realize that when we are living by faith, and nothing very much is happening, we are being searched by God in our inmost being and tested by him, without the benefit of any signposts. My part is to be open to him, still as still, no doubt, without too much rushing round, accepting the work of God in me. Then he lifts me in knowledge so that though I do not see clearly, I understand the looking-glass principle, and I can at least see that my values have been turned upside down, and rightly. So it is God who is doing the revolutionary things in me, rather than myself doing revolutionary things. It is God who is turning me upside down, back to front.

All this is experienced by going through Christ and remaining in Christ, being with Christ. But each of us has to experience as of now and in the future. We will be at different stages from other people. But it is not important to know where you are . . . indeed it is more important to experience and live out that you do *not* know where you are!

I suppose my sense of this doorway to God finds interesting backing not only from Alice, but from a number of science fiction writers. One writer for instance, Robert Heinlein, uses the title *Tunnel in the Sky* to describe a time and space jump through a 'gate'; and there are many others who stretch the mind similarly. Not all such writings especially parallel the experience of going through Christ, but a closer parallel does come in a story called *Commencement Night* by Richard Ashby. It is a story of young people isolated on an island from all adult human contact. They are visited by Eren Tu, a person from another world, through whose 'system' they develop amazingly. Then an adult (Ted) is introduced by a particular child (Lute) to the 'system'. Lute

'gazed up into Ted's eyes and began giving him certain curious instructions, the very formulation and expression of which were possible only because of the fluidity and precision of the island language. Ted was made partially to blank his mind and to let the sensation of pain settle into a particular area. When it had coalesced and settled down, Lute gave him what amounted to the form and dimensions of his identity-extensions. A corner of his thoughts found time to rebel in admiration: orthodox mind science would probably have gone on missing the simplicity that was the essence of individual identity for a thousand years . . .

The pain vanished. And with his smile of pleasure came an indescribable mixture of emotions; peace was there, but it was a thrilling and dynamic thing, not placidity. A strength and courage such as he had never before known seemed to be his now, and a burning desire to use his vigour to live and experience and to be.

He was in love. With everything.

"Don't you see," he shouted at the bewildered Eren Tu, "I'm whole, I'm well, I'm as I was probably intended to be . . . This is what my planet's religious men have been trying to speak of. But without knowing it for themselves, and without a language to teach it, they made it into a soggy, revolting piety. This is *love*, and I'm operating *from* it."

"Can others make the change-over?"

"Why not? Certainly. Anyone that speaks the island tongue. There are thousands of us." . . .

Eren Tu, the man from the stars, shook his head. "Apparently there's only one way of finding out for sure. If they make the change—".'

It is very true that within the Church we can and often do give a soggy sense rather than the crisp, dynamic vision and life of Jesus Christ. But his teaching and example open mind and heart, because they open him as door. But the only way of finding this out for sure is by going through the door, with all that this implies.

At the beginning of this chapter, we noticed that the setting of the passage we are pondering on was the story of the man born blind whom Jesus cured. This associates it with blindness and seeing, with darkness and light. The man himself came through the doorway in two senses.

Physically, for the first time he saw the world, people, and Jesus Christ. Spiritually, seeing and believing with the eyes of faith, he saw Jesus Christ as the Son of man: 'Jesus said, "Do you believe in the Son of man?" He answered, "And who is he, sir, that I may believe in him?" Jesus said to him, "You have seen him, and it is he who speaks with you." He said, "Lord, I believe", and he worshipped him.' (*John 9.35–38*)

It is tantalizing that we are not told what happened after that, but it is clear from those few words that a whole new way of life opened up, when he passed through the door of faith. Take two aspects.

Firstly, having passed through, the cured man (or you and I) worshipped. Now, worship, public or private, is the setting for re-orientation, for adjusting to 'the other side', for living in the looking-glass world. To be there in worship, in faith, is to step forward into the unknown future of God's creation. As such, because we worship the im-mense-unknown-known, we have to worship from humility, with the courage which we need to step through any doorway to the future. Jesus, when he spoke to the woman at the well in John chapter 4 said: 'The hour is coming, and now is, when the true worshippers will worship the Father in spirit and in truth, for such the Father seeks to worship him. God is spirit, and those who worship him must worship in spirit and truth.' To be true to the new realization, the cured man worshipped. If as I hope, we come through the door, we too must worship.

Secondly, in coming through, his new vision put him at odds with those who had not even noticed that the door was a door, and so had not gone through. If, as I hope, we know the door and pass through, this very action may set us at a difference with those who by all logic should know better than us. Here is a problem and a test . . . to keep stepping forward against the warnings of the wise, be-cause of the vision. This demands from us trust and humility, and these in turn come from worship.

But perhaps one of the things we find ourselves most

lacking is confidence when we approach these seemingly dark and deep areas. We would therefore be wrong if we did not remember in the same imagery that Jesus himself did not only demand 'the hard thing', but also gave a lot of encouragement and hope. In what is surely a classic statement of the combination of Christ both boosting morale and also warning about 'the hard thing', Matthew tells us: 'Ask, and it will be given to you; search, and you will find; knock, and the door will be opened to you. For the one who asks always receives; the one who searches always finds; the one who knocks will always have the door opened to him.... Enter by the narrow gate, since the room that leads to perdition is wide and spacious, and many take it; but it is a narrow gate and a hard road that leads to life, and only a few find it.' (*Matt.* 7.7–14)

It is, perhaps, this combination which is the effective mixture as far as the human being is concerned. In other words, by our very nature we only really fully grow and develop if we have a rich blending of joy and sorrow, pain and delight, acceptance and rejection, knowledge and darkness of mind. And in this, what is really the crucial point is the coming together of a free will in man and the free Spirit of God, which only fully happens if man steps forward voluntarily and in faith through the door to meet the Spirit of Love. To step forward against one's will and without love is to meet the Spirit of love in blindness, bitterness and even hatred, and so to lose oneself – not in love – but in disintegration.

This is a process which continues throughout life, until we step through death into eternity. The culminating stage is illustrated in the account given in C. S. Lewis' *The Last Battle* of the final hours of Narnia and the judgement of the Talking Beasts:

> Obviously, unless either the Door had grown very much larger or the creatures had suddenly grown as small as gnats, a crowd like that couldn't ever have tried to get through it ...

The creatures came rushing on, their eyes brighter and brighter as they drew nearer and nearer to the standing Stars. But as they came right up to Aslan one or other of two things happened to each of them. They all looked straight in his face; I don't think they had any other choice about that. And when some looked, the expression of their faces changed terribly – it was fear and hatred: except that, on the faces of the Talking Beasts, the fear and hatred only lasted for a fraction of a second. You could see that they suddenly ceased to be *Talking* Beasts. They were just ordinary animals. And all the creatures who looked at Aslan in that way swerved to their right, his left, and disappeared in his huge black shadow, which, as you have heard, streamed away to the left of the doorway. The children never saw them again. I don't know what became of them. But the others looked in the face of Aslan and loved him, though some of these were very frightened at the same time. And all these came in at the Door, in on Aslan's right. There were some queer specimens among them.

So, to sum up, let us remember we use the phrase: 'to go through life'. It is as though life was a continuous door such as appears in a hall of mirrors, when you stand and see the continuous reproduction caused by reflection of one mirror on another. Each step we take, each day we enter is a new experience in a new world. If we are blessed in prayer, we realize at some point that each door we go through is in reality a person, and we meet and go through Jesus Christ. If we are less fortunate, we may not consciously meet Jesus the Door, and so it may be the coming of death and the final judgement which bring us face to face with the reality. But whether we are conscious of him or not, we should always step forward in faith that the door we do not even see will be opened to us.

4

I AM THE VINE . . . YOU ARE THE BRANCHES

> I am the vine,
> you are the branches. (*John 15.5*)

The people to whom Jesus and his immediate followers were talking lived and moved in vine country; they were Mediterranean people. The impact of the vine image was naturally more immediate for them (and still is for numerous inhabitants of wine-producing countries), than for people used to urban living and a northern climate. Indeed, talk to my parishioners today, and the only grapes they have ever seen are in shops, while wine for them simply comes out of a bottle; a vine is something outside their experience.

I have known some Christians therefore write off the phrase attributed to Jesus, 'I am the vine, you are the branches', as useless for meditation and instruction today. Such dismissal is too swift. To be sure, it is necessary and urgent that those deeply committed to spreading the word of God should devote themselves to translating the essential meaning of Christ's message into ideas and language which are readily understandable today. But we must guard against a development, perhaps associated with books, colleges, church buildings and so on, which grows so far away from the original portrayal that it is quite beyond what the majority can understand. Thus there emerge select groups within the Church and the churches which speak and live out a specialist language, and impose it on others. (Do you and I already belong to such groups?)

In any event, the 'common man' still has a need, whether it is recognized or not, to take a serious look at the old, at the original presentation of Jesus, and see what depth he can discover in it if he will only give a little time, patience and effort. (Somewhat similarly, men can still gain so much from encountering the classics of drama, music, painting or literature, and these in their original form, for all the up-dating and the fresh modes of expression that modern times bring forth.) Anyone who is a Christian, and wants to be genuinely committed to Christ, will yearn to know with the whole of his being who Jesus Christ is. He must be prepared to sit with the New Testament images, to think, wonder and contemplate.

The theme song repeated again and again in *Jesus Christ Superstar*, a modern interpretation which has had a mixed reception, is: 'Who are you? What are you? Jesus Christ – Superstar.' Though such a cry may not be acceptable to you personally, it is as real in our society today as was the cry John the Baptist sent out from prison: 'Are you the one who is to come, or must we wait for someone else?' Our trouble to some extent is that we tend to have grown up with Jesus Christ, or received him in the past. We are on one level familiar with him, and we remain superficial in our relationship, and edit it to our needs. Our practice, in groups, church communities, families, and on our own, should be to discuss and ponder, pray over and listen to, Jesus Christ.

What then can be made of Jesus' statement: 'I am the vine, you are the branches'? Initially, our minds can play over various images of limbs drawing life from some central core: branches in relation to vine, to oak tree, or again, to head office; arms or legs in relation to the whole body. For me now, although only after a considerable time, the idea of Christ as vine means something very real, very deep. I find myself linking it closely with 'I am the way, the truth and the life', and especially with 'the life'.

We may recall the basic statement of Jesus Christ, 'Without me you can do nothing.' Now the thinking of Christians goes through periods and phases, which reflect something of the contemporary man and his needs. There have been times when there was a lot of worry and opposition among Christians against those who developed the notion and method of stillness in prayer and waiting on God. Activity vies with stillness. A characteristic tendency in this country is to have a deep-set sense of the need to achieve our own salvation, by our own efforts – a tendency no doubt inherited from Pelagius.

We are all as individuals very different, and how right and healthy it is that there should be every variety of approach. But in all of us there is a need for some degree of balance between exploitation of our active nature and relaxing, keeping still, contemplating. Jesus' theme 'Without me you can do nothing' has been useful to me in viewing this balance. And we can explore this same theme by invoking the example of the vine and the branches. For the branch can only have life fully when fully living in the vine and from the vine's life. There is nothing the branch can do for itself, since all the growth from the first shooting comes from the main stem of the vine. In this way, it could be said that the branch is passive and relies totally on the surge of life-blood sap rising in the vine. The growth which results stretches out further and further from the main stem, and should eventually bear fruit. Of course, there are dangers of blight or frost or tempestuous wind, but the internal growth-power remains so long as the branch is attached and the vine is alive. The growth-power is internal. No matter what external stimulus there may be, unless the internal life is circulating, there will be no fruit.

The simplicity of the concept of vine and branches is for me best summed up in Paul's words: 'I live now not I but Christ lives in me.' The truth of this statement, and its reality in my life, took a long time to penetrate. Has it penetrated you?

In some ways another image, that of the shoot being grafted on to the vine, is more vivid, because once the grafting (Baptism) has taken place, we are brought to share Christ's life in the resurrection. Where we attempt to do too much on our own, we ignore the reality that Christ lives in us, and we impose a separate and wrong idea that it is us that must reach out to God, and get ourselves close to him. That is as though the branch of the vine were to stretch out to the sun, while disregarding totally the source of life inside itself!

Jesus' teaching, then, is that he really lives in us. No multitude of words can go beyond this teaching. Once again, we need to sit in wonder, letting the message seep through our being, feeling the life growing through us. Then, in a realization which will constantly need re-awakening as we go on, we can stretch out to live Christ's life in the world.

Although the strength and simplicity of this truth have been taught in all the ages of Christianity, the human element and our worldly education do what they can to obscure the truth. We are educated to stand on our own feet, to fight our way to the top. The rat race is on, and adults already involved in it, bring their children up in the same direction. Even when we genuinely believe that we intend to teach them a Godward path, a God-centred life, we work away at contradicting this in so many attitudes in and out of church, which accept the here-and-now fact that children must be educated for work, for a wage or salary, for life here in a materialistic age. By stressing the requirements of examinations and qualifications we lead many to the sheer accumulation of facts, rather than to a growth of thought and wonder, an ability to be still, an understanding of stillness, an appreciation of the innerness of man.

Let us then go back to this inner life. Presuming for the moment that you are baptised, and that – however strong or weak in faith and practice – you are a believer, then God is not only with you but in you. The growth of this as true in us is a growth of realization of this same truth. The relationship which for me already exists is more powerful and more developed in the degree that it is real to me. This does not mean that I have a constant and tangible sense of it, but that it is real. I can explain this best through a delightful quotation from Margery Williams' children's story: *The Velveteen Rabbit*:

'What is real?' asked the rabbit one day when they were lying side by side near the nursery fender, before Nama came to tidy the room. 'Does it mean having things that buzz inside you and a stick out handle?'

'Real isn't how you are made,' said the Skin Horse. 'It's a thing that happens to you. When a child loves you for a long, long time, not just to play with, but REALLY loves you, then you become REAL.'

'Does it hurt?' asked the Rabbit.

'Sometimes,' said the Skin Horse, for he was always truthful. 'When you are Real you don't mind being hurt.'

'Does it happen all at once, like being wound up,' he asked, 'or bit by bit?'

'It doesn't happen all at once,' said the Skin Horse. 'You become. It takes a long time. That's why it doesn't often happen to people who break easily, or have sharp edges, or who have to be carefully kept. Generally, by the time you are Real, most of your hair has been loved off, and your eyes drop out and you get loose in the joints and very shabby. But these things don't matter at all, because once you are Real you can't be ugly, except to people who don't understand.'

'I suppose you are Real?' said the Rabbit. And then he wished he had not said it, for he thought the Skin Horse might be sensitive. But the Skin Horse only smiled.

'The Boy's Uncle made me Real,' he said. 'That was a great many years ago, but once you are Real you can't become unreal again. It lasts for always.'

It is in this sense that after Baptism we grow in reality. At any given moment we are as full of life as we are; but the potential growth is beyond our limits of understanding. We become more and more real, that is more and more full of Christ-life as we live out and grow out the truth of his life in us. It is from this that fruit comes.

Therefore, we are not completely passive, but are open to the flow of his life, and are willing and working to use that life to the full.

At this point, it becomes clearer how a further development of the vine theme is applicable. Life is made up of seasons. We are not likely to grow unless we accept the cold and heat, spring and autumn, whatever form those may take not only in the weather, but in the depth of our whole being. The sap, the life of God, does not always seem to course through us at the same rate. At times we feel lifeless, abandoned; at other times we are bursting with belief, and hope and love and action.

What is more, we grow fruitful from pruning. We can see this in the case of the vine. We are far less able to see it in our own case. We lose a friend, we have an accident, we make a mess of something. There is always a possibility that we will simply fail to see that corners need knocking off, or that a loss of pride can be a growth in humility. Look round history at the great changes which have come to people in ways which at the time seemed cruel, brutal, unloving. yet which looking back are the real growth-point of character.

Living through the problem of pain, which tears at man's belief in a good God, is part of what it takes to make us real. Now to me another point of growth was the realization that Jesus Christ himself was not outside this human necessity of growth through pain. To me it is powerfully filled with meaning that Jesus grew, knew the bitterness of lack of response, knew what it was to be too busy to talk to his friends, got tired and had to rest at the well, and still had to give. That he wasn't followed; that

47

his followers misunderstood what was involved, that they deserted him; that he was literally beaten, spat upon, harried on the way to the cross, and knew what it is to die ... all this is powerful in my life. For he did not only do it as an example. His message spelt out in the years of his life is, starkly: I, Son of God, living in man suffer in the general sense all that a man suffers, including death. You then, man-woman-child, you go through the same because it is all somehow included in the plan of my Father-God. Now, I live in you, man, and surely you expect to grow as I have grown in man, through living, through loving, through suffering and through dying?

In the life of Christ, some of the pruning was externally determined – the way he was born and grew, exile in Egypt, the limitations of his background, education and human nature. Other parts were self-imposed discipline – nights in prayer, forty days' fast and watch in the desert, setting his face to Jerusalem. He had to take himself in hand, led by the Spirit, against the temptations of the evil one and of his friends also. Is it not encouraging and helpful to consider that he foreknew that Peter would have to be sifted like chaff, until he was ready to confirm his brethren in a newfound strength which grew from sifting, pruning. The very admonition of Christ that a follower of his takes up his cross, is a call to self-discipline.

If we face the Christian life and somehow think we can get away with it without suffering and self-discipline and sorrow, and pruning from outside as well – then we are committing intense self-deception. And unfortunately there will not only be deception of ourselves but of others who are led to think this is the Christian life we are living. This statement by itself may be overharsh, for it would be unbalanced to think all was tears and pain and sorrow in following Jesus. Rather than that, we need to remember that his yoke is sweet, his burden light, and the gift he brings is peace and joy. The riddle of this mingling in any one life, and in church society, is the riddle of Christ himself – once more a mystery to be pondered, contemplated; a mystery not wholly subject to human reasoning.

The imposition of self-discipline which is most easily understood in relation to the vine image is therefore to me twofold. Firstly, it is the discipline of leaving myself open to the Lord, open to the Spirit, so that the very sap, the very life may flow through me. Only in this way will growth come. But how do I leave myself open? This is a question for each individual. The only foundation hints I can give from experience are as follows:

> Be regular, day by day, in setting aside time for prayer. Let this time be open to the Spirit . . . not cluttered with thought.

> Whatever your fears, hold yourself there. Let God work on you, no matter where he leads you.

In this way the vine-life, Jesus, the Spirit, will rise in you.

Secondly, and growing from this, it is the discipline of leaving oneself open to people. The only way the fruit of the vine is of any use is if it is picked, and eaten or used for drink. If the fruit remains on the branch, it is beautiful but useless except for the human eye – and eventually it will die, shrivelled. In a very terrible passage, which becomes a nightmare for the preacher, Christ curses the fig tree which is barren. I find it terrifying because the story is mysterious, as is Christ. And I know deep inside me that I can often find excuses for not bringing forth fruit, which are fine in my eyes, until I look straight at Jesus Christ, and then I begin to realize that what I want to do is preserve my fruit, myself; I don't want always to be given to others, to be picked and eaten up. Yet Jesus not only has the zeal of the Lord eating him up, but he makes himself so available that he has no time of his own; and he ends by making himself available in the Eucharist, telling us to eat him and drink him and live by him.

No one will cultivate a vine without hope of grapes. Why should the Father, the vine-dresser, cultivate you, if you are not bearing fruit? Or if, bearing fruit, you will not share it, your very life, with others, following Christ's lead?

I think the combination of these two points of self-discipline, practised over a period of time, which is a life time, make up what it is to be real. In the course of it, you will be drained again and again. You will become old and tattered; you will become beautiful a very different way from Miss World. But your beauty will be real with the reality of Jesus Christ crucified, who went through it all before he became glorious, and part of whose glory shone in the very scars of human life and death. To be real is to be really alive. For us, really alive must mean really alive in Christ.

Much of this is applicable at first on the level of the individual. I think it would be wrong to keep it so, and not to recognize the group, body or community aspect, for this is central to the concept of the vine and branches, and is for us a very necessary part of Christianity, though one sadly neglected in so many parishes. The opportunity will vary, but each of us should take a long hard look at ourselves and our community to sum up for ourselves what we are attempting, what we are achieving and what we are lacking.

As there is no branch without the vine, there is no Christianity without Christ. What we should consider carefully is how much Christianity there is without the Church. It is a very large question, and today there is a powerful challenge from those who do not want or see the relevance of organized or institutional religion. I just put forward my view, which you may well want to discuss or contradict, that the Church is necessary for Christianity. A lone man, refusing fellowship with other Christians, is in that refusal missing out on an essential element of Christianity, namely that of gathered people. However inhibiting, however lacking in the fullness of actual Christian living a local church may be, the concept Church, the people of God, with some form of link between them is to me essential. I know there could be much discussion here. I know that writing as a Roman Catholic I may think and speak differently from members of other Christian Churches; I may even speak differently from some members of my own Church ... but I am still adamant in saying that I consider membership of Church as essential. This does not mean that from the viewpoint of the Church authorities I am always saying one hundred per cent what they think I should be saying. Indeed, I believe that there are times when individuals have to speak out against what is being said or done, and I believe the Church herself knows there is always need of reform in her as there is in the individual. But for me, the cohesion in the vine, the continued membership of the Church is eaten right into my being. The more deeply I find myself involved with Christ, the more deeply I find myself involved with Church, though it is not always a passive, easy relationship.

I remember reading once the summing up of what it was like to have a particular fairly turbulent, lively and holy Dominican friar in a community. He was Vincent McNabb, who preached very often at Hyde Park corner in the earlier part of this century. His one-time superior wrote: Having him in the community was like having a lion on a string – but the string never broke.

To me our Christian community living is too often made up of pussies and doves – the pussies sometimes getting catty and the doves flying away in disorder, and nothing being achieved for Christ.

Rather than this, it is our part to try to build community in our area. In this, by ingrafting others, we can have a healing role in society. Strengthening others by our fellowship and love, we can help them to grow together and bear fruit. By sharing ideas, vitality, homes, interests and widening concern for others, we can broaden our own capacity for caring actively.

If we were to employ our imagination on a fanciful portrait of the fruitful vine, then we could visualize it as gathering all its life and strength together, urging the branches on to giving forth more and more clusters of grapes, and by their very being and attractive appearance tempting those beyond the vine to 'taste and see how sweet'. This virtually is the mission of the Christian, by being ever more full of the Spirit and alive in Christ, to show forth the fruits – love, joy, peace, patience and so on.

Yet here we must pause and examine our individual and collective conscience. Is this the appearance which comes from us to those around; are we lights to enlighten, or glooms to cloud the vision?

Jesus Christ's example and I can only call it 'inspiration' was that he was incarnate, that he became man and dwelt among us. Study this very simply in relation to your situation today. Jesus lived on earth and in the midst of his people. He did not live in a palace, he did not move out to a select suburb of Jerusalem. He lived in Nazareth, which from the words of Nicodemus was a despised little place ... 'can anything good come out of Nazareth', he said. What was more, as he went on living and preaching, he still stayed among his people. He did not get removed or alienated from their condition, except that he perhaps became poorer and less secure than they, without anywhere to lay his head.

Christians could well sit down and think out how we/they are allowing the world to develop. There is what is in modern jargon called polarization – the richer people move into richer suburbs and the countryside and special areas, while other areas, generally in cities, become lower and lower in their standard of housing and living. These latter areas then find that doctors, lawyers, teachers, welfare and social workers, and even the police serving them tend to make their homes away from their place of work, which itself is too tough, or simply not good enough, for them.

Unthinkingly, Christians are going along with this, becoming more middle/upper class, and going back to the more Victorian ideas of 'do-gooding' ... that is, visiting into an area to help in the day, or once or twice a week, and then moving out to home, leaving the problems till next day.

I would like earnest consideration of this, leading to a more active policy among Christians for keeping the Christian life incarnational. By this I mean that we should make efforts to train ourselves to live scattered through the general community, accepting our responsibility locally, being a leaven ... accepting that the vine is there locally and we must not detach ourselves to some more salubrious vineyard, but help with the more arid areas, the less attractive parts of towns and cities. I know there are some who are doing this already; but the call of Jesus Christ is much more incarnational than this, much wider in its application, if we are to give life, Christ life, where it is so badly needed.

Reading this, you could well go away and say to yourself: this man is writing pie-in-the-sky stuff ... idealistic ... out of this world. Right ... it probably is. But I would want you to stop and sit for a moment over my reply, which is: If you are professing to follow Jesus Christ, you are following an idealist; if you are claiming to be a Christian, might not that commit you to being 'out of this world', if once you gauge your standard and mode of living by that of Jesus himself?

5

I AM THE GOOD SHEPHERD

But who wants to be a sheep, anyhow?

I have heard this kind of objection to Christ, to Christianity and to the working of the Church again and again. A sheep, we feel, is a silly senseless animal, one of a herd, directed and swayed by external influence rather than by inner purpose. And have not precisely these features been evident among believers – and perhaps been deliberately fostered – time and again in Christian history? If I am honest with myself and with whoever is raising this objection, I must admit that it has my heartfelt sympathy. But then I want to go on and reconsider the whole matter, to see whether I am taking a sufficiently balanced and penetrating view of it.

Let us think first of the shepherd role as a leadership role, with the sheep correspondingly as those who are led.

Perhaps there is in most of us a combination of urges. In some areas we all want to be shepherds; in other areas we are content to be sheep; while in other areas again we grumble and object at being cast as sheep, but are not willing to stir ourselves to the action and responsibility which would be involved in changing ourselves into shepherds. If for example we look at the role of the ordinary citizen in local elections, we find a massive inertia: no scramble to be a local councillor or even to vote for one. The same is true in Trade Unions, where it is normal for a tiny minority to sway the shop floor. Becoming more parochial, the same is true in church councils and so on ... with plenty of gossip and expressed irritation, but little volunteering of action.

The Church in its more monolithic forms has tended to accentuate and petrify the structure of shepherd and sheep through various forms of hierarchy which, practically speaking, place power in a few hands and leave the main body merely acquiescing, often without much knowledge of what is going on. The less hierarchical churches are in a sense a reaction against this process, and to some extent they have maintained a greater overall responsibility among the laity.

In the kingdom of Israel the shepherd was a father figure, one might say; his shepherding including not only flocks of animals but the flock of his family, tribe and whole people.

But how close is any of this to that leadership with which Christ was concerned, which is expressed in the imagery of shepherd and sheep? We must recall again that Jesus and his disciples do not use empty words and pictures. So if you feel awkward about this imagery, and tempted to reject the whole idea, it would be wise for you to stop, take another look, and see whether the qualities explicit in Jesus' words about the shepherd, and implicit in his whole way of life, are at all similar to *your* understanding of the leadership evoked by 'shepherd'. To start with, read through John 10.1–18, and think deeply about the succession of points Jesus makes so clearly . . . take your time, and then we can reflect on them together. . .

. . . The first startling revelation we come across is he knows his sheep by name. This is startling, because we each of us realize in ourselves just how much we like to be known. It goes through all levels of our relationship, the depth depending on closeness. We expect our parents, relations and friends to know our names, we get flattered when someone 'big' knows us; we get fed up and angry when we are not remembered, because we become insignificant, we 'lose' our 'self'. It is incredible to some people that God should know us, know me. Out of all the myriads of galaxies, he knows earth; out of all the teeming millions on earth . . . me. Incredible!

I find I can sit and just wonder at that, and wonder! He knows my name, he knows me. And that not just casually, but in the true deep sense of 'knowing' which also includes loving. It is on this basis that trust is set up, for he not only knows, but he is known. So my part in the relationship is set up, and I find myself realizing that his side is always there and open and effective: he always does and always will know my name. But on my side, I am quite able to forget his name; I am quite able to get fed up with the relationship; I am quite capable of getting lost.

When I accept him and know him, his leadership can come into play. And what is this leadership? It is very literal: 'The sheep hear his voice, and he calls his own sheep by name and leads them out.' It is difficult for Jesus, granting that he has made us free, to lead us out on any other basis than that of his knowing us and our knowing and being drawn to him. There have been long ages of commandments, threats and penalties in a dire and rather negative fashion . . . Do this, or you will go to Hell; don't do that, or you will go to Hell. And all the time, the command has really been positive – Love God, Love your neighbour . . . and, in Jesus' own words: 'Follow me.'

This puts me right back, or forward, into the absolute necessity of doing all I can on my side to deepen and widen my knowledge and love of God in Christ by prayer, meditation, listening, contemplation and the living out of what I learn.

My trust must be great, because he is 'leading me out'. The very notion of 'out' sends shudders down the spine, with all its implications of coldness, lack of security and danger. But the constant message of Jesus is the assurance of his presence: 'He goes before them, and the sheep follow him, for they know his voice.' It is the same assurance as the I AM – I WILL BE THERE.

He will be there . . . out in front, for he has always gone ahead in living his life in this world to the end. Though he has not encountered in his own experience each single incident which can befall any one of us, he has lived out a life, and that is as much as any human being is asked to do: he has lived it out in obedience to his Father's will, and that too is what the human is asked to do; finally he has lived it out in love to the extent of laying down his life for his sheep – and all we humans are asked to do the same.

The truth dawns that we are all supposed to be leaders, just as Christ was a leader. It is at this point that those of us who do not feel we are much in the way of leaders start jogging our visible leaders and at the same time holding back ourselves; while not a few leaders find that it was much more comfortable to lead when they were not out in front, and now that they supposedly ought to be out there, it is easier and less dangerous to shy back and 'lead' from the rear. I can only say to ourselves and to them that Jesus Christ got out in front, he was fearless though he was overcome with fear, he did not shrink back, although he did shrink back. That is the example the Good Shepherd gave his sheep.

It should, I think, be easy for each of us to stop a minute and think over some of the true leaders whom we have had among Christians in this century, especially quite recently. We may note that while there have been a considerable number who have been outstanding, what might be called 'general leadership' has not been significant, especially in regard to living the harder aspects of Christianity. In considering and assessing the various leaders, it would be well to analyse the individual qualities we recognize in them, and then think back to the Good Shepherd.

But here again, if we are not careful, we shall find that we are building for ourselves a nice cosy position from which to criticize, whereas we are the very ones who should be out in the lead ... ourselves. I view our situation this way.

Jesus' disciples were sent out on a limited mission during his lifetime, the mission of the seventy-two. But

57

then they returned to the 'sheep' role until after the Resurrection, when Peter specifically was told to feed the lambs and the sheep. And after Pentecost we find all the apostles doing this very thing in their living, preaching and healing. Then they had to gather others to help them; and with the spread of small communities in the Mediterranean area, more and more leaders emerged from among the ordinary people, sometimes from very recent converts to Christ.

So the marvellous thing about Jesus was that he led as far as he needed to, including to some extent in a paternal way, and then left his disciples to do the work of leading others, a work in which he calls on us today to share. In this he showed his great trust for the very untrustworthy us. How sad it is that we in comparison have so little trust in ourselves and each other!

This trust Jesus showed is tied up with the intimate knowledge he had of his disciples. He knew their strengths and weaknesses; he knew just how unreliable they were; and yet taking all this into consideration, he trusted them with his life and his work. And he treats *us* likewise.

If I can sit in undisguised wonder at the thought that Jesus knows me, I find myself in still greater wonder that, knowing me ... he trusts me! When I do not even trust myself, he trusts me. When I am over-trusting of myself and my capabilities, and fall flat on my face in failure, he trusts me.

The upshot of all this is that Jesus has left us now – all who are baptised into his body, and not just ministers or bishops – to be shepherds and not merely sheep. Baptism itself and Confirmation too put us into the role of shepherds, because the moment that we 'know' Jesus Christ, we have a responsibility for spreading that knowledge. Unhappily, we do not by any means all take the opportunity and discharge the duty which is presented to us ... in other words we are not so committed to Christ as he would have us be. Once more, we like to be sheep at this point, though quickly ready to criticize the ineffectiveness of our leaders.

Perhaps each of us should pause here and put a few questions to ourselves. In what sense do we consider ourselves as 'pastors'? How far do we evade such responsibility and push it off to those conceived as 'dedicated' to God's service in a specialist way? Indeed, do we accept as correct the notion of our having any pastoral responsibility at all?

What a Christ-mad idea to take sheep and make them shepherds! But in its way, is this any more strange than taking a prostitute and making her on a level with virgins, taking a tax-collector and making him an apostle, taking you and me and making us saints?

Christ-mad or not: this is Christ-fact!

Let us now look at a further aspect of Christ's life which is conveyed in the shepherd/sheep image, namely his particular concern for people who are lost. This takes us somewhat beyond the passage from John referred to earlier. Perhaps the most immediately vivid picture for us here is that of the widow who loses one coin out of her savings and, though she has the rest, turns her house upside down until she finds it, and then is quite disproportionately overjoyed at recovering it. We have all been through this kind of thing at some time or another. Probably not so immediate for most of us, but more in keeping with our present theme, is the story of the lost sheep. We recall how the shepherd leaves ninety-nine in the flock and goes out to seek, in order to save, the one which is lost.

Many people today are specialists. If we were to think of Jesus Christ as having a particular specialization, what would you say it was? Pause and consider that for a minute or two . . . don't just read on . . . and then see if we are thinking along the same lines . . .

I think he was a specialist in lost persons; and I think this characteristic specialization is powerfully expressed in the idea of the Good Shepherd. It may seem strange that having emphasized the 'knowing' element in the shepherd/sheep relationship, I now switch to the 'lost' aspect. But this is important: for if we are hesitant to admit and in turn to assume the role of shepherd, we are likely to be even more hesitant to accept that the shepherd in Christ's lesson to us is more interested in the sinner than in the just, in those who feel lost than in those who feel at home or saved.

It is sometimes sneeringly suggested that the God in whom Christians believe has no general relevance to modern man, and only comes in in crises and lost causes: a sort of humanitarian 'God of the gaps'! This is a quite different picture to the one given by Jesus himself, because he draws in *all* men to himself. None the less it is clear that his particular purpose is to seek out the lost. At first this seems confined to 'the lost sheep of Israel', but gradually it is extended, without losing the emphasis on the lost.

Now a basic Christian belief is in 'justification', in the sense of fastening on to the saving power of Christ. The danger is that before we know where we are we have become an exclusive group or body, with little genuine personal concern for those who in one way or another appear to us as 'outsiders'. Keeping the right balance here is extremely hard; it is a balance which may not always be understood even among the 'just'. Jesus himself, of course, came under heavy fire for eating with publicans and sinners, for talking to Samaritans, for consorting with prostitutes, for having riff-raff as friends.

Moreover while there were some cases of a change of heart among individuals of this type, there is no indication that Jesus had a general success, that he was recognized as a 'successful social worker'. But then, his purpose was not simply on the social work level, for he was always leading out into a fuller life, one which would be whole, in the sense of body, mind, soul, the entire individual, living a full life in relationship to God, self and others.

The physical healing of a leper by itself was not what Christ was about. He wanted the leper to recognize him, to thank him, and to continue that thanks by praising God. He did not forgive the woman taken in adultery merely because eventually no one else stayed to condemn her; he was interested in her aftercare ... Go and sin no more. And if we accept her as Mary Magdalen, then we know that the effect was a lasting rehabilitation, which could only have been achieved through his lasting care and concern. Each of the miracles and outstanding events in Jesus' life which deal with the poor, the lost, the abandoned, bring new life and hope.

I think very serious consideration of this aspect of the Good Shepherd is of paramount importance today if we are to accept the role of the shepherd leading us out. Out from where? Out in the first place from our rather enclosed sense of Church, out from our rather 'nice' behaviour and into the open challenge and danger of life in the world. Parallel to Jesus, our call is first to the 'lost' of the new Israel, the Christian Church. And we must assess in what this 'lostness' consists. For it often lies in the fact that the voice of Jesus has *itself* been muffled or lost in its communication by the shepherds of today (you and I). In this direction, we must not only pray for wise and courageous leadership in the manner of Jesus, but we must ourselves get out to lead with a lot more commitment and conviction. We must always be clear, however, that we cannot browbeat people back into belief. Like the Good Shepherd, we can only *lead* them: and they may not actually come! So we need patience and perseverance, both of which are surely characteristic of the action of God in Christ? But we need also honesty in looking straight at the criticisms, and alleged reasons for fall-away, so that we can try to right what is wrong in us and in our communication of Christ, and at the same time speak gently but directly to blindness or refusal to accept, where we see fault on the side of the 'lost' person.

Christ shows us the perseverance he has with Scribes

and Pharisees in opening up his truth to them; he demonstrates in the Good Thief how even the last moment is not too late; he reminds us in the parable of the prodigal son that the father is waiting all the time in his son's prolonged lapse. Watching these and other episodes in Christ's life, let us hold a mirror to ourselves in anything like the same long-drawn-out situation. Do we appreciate that our work with any one individual may be a lifetime work: not just this week or next week, or even next year, but perhaps five years, ten years, twenty ... and still no change, no response! Is one prepared to wait and help, hope and watch, pray and love through ... nothing?

So far I have been writing of my or your attitude on the basis that we have faith and are trying to live it, and have to that extent been 'found' by God. What about the other way round? What about the 'lost' person, if you happen to be one? Here, I think the great hope that Jesus offers, although it is not in a sense much consolation or a way of escape, is simply that this is not unnatural or unlikely. It is very normal. 'Lostness' does not mean damnation or hopelessness: or at least, it doesn't mean the former and shouldn't mean the latter! Some may have brought lostness on themselves and may feel guilty. Look up then and recognize that Jesus is waiting for you, because he really meant it when he said he laid down his life for his sheep, and coupled this with having come for the lost sheep. Even if lostness is your fault, he does not exclude you. Try to accept that you must not exclude yourself, by judging wrongly that you are excluded.

I find one of the very hardest things there is to do is reconciling a person who feels cut off, and has somehow become determined that there is nothing you, I or God can do about it. This last conclusion is quite contrary to Christ's attitude. If you have it, blank your mind and heart to the past, open forward to Jesus, and accept, accept, accept!

In the middle of writing this, I visited a long-term, high-security prison. Going in is to me enormously depressing, and always makes me feel guilty. And within, though some have found faith and hope, for many there is a bleak sense of emptiness and future hopelessness expressing the feeling that no one can help. But this still leaves room for the work of God, hard though that work may be. And this is all the more reason to visit the imprisoned, so that they may hope again . . . and to spread more compassion among ourselves outside, so that re-entry to the 'free' world may be made easier when the time comes.

Though externally, it may be said in accusation that the Church is very hard with its power to 'bind and loose', and that a person may cut himself off from Church society and membership, in practice there are comparatively few instances where this need happen permanently. For there are a great many ways to reconciliation, if only those who are working in this field had the time and patience to investigate. I am sure pastors and counsellors and just ordinary men and women could have a very great ministry in healing, freeing and reconciling – much greater that is than appears today. But it needs a combination of depth of faith and prayer alongside breadth, firmness, tolerance and sympathy, love and patience.

To carry on the thought of captivity and freedom, and to move out from the circle of believers or one-time believers, we could think briefly of those in our general society who in their own way are lost and perhaps unable to be reconciled with society. There are many, many of them; one section with whom I have been particularly closely involved while writing this has been the gypsies, or as they are sometimes called 'the Travellers'. It would not be too hard on the average Christian to guess that reaction to the presence of gypsies camped in the neighbourhood would be one of rising heat and a sense of grievance that they should be allowed to stay there. The reaction might well continue that they were dirty, left everything in a mess, were light-fingered and a general nuisance, and that 'something should be done about them'. But how concerned are we for the needs of the gypsies themselves? How far do we see them merely as threats to our own way of life? I wonder how many Christians are much aware of the problems gypsies face and the way they are harried by society. While one may well try to help towards rehabilitation (or perhaps better 'habilitation'), it is useful to reflect on an analogy which a member of their Council with whom I was recently working used to highlight the problem of attempting to make gypsies settle down. You cannot immediately cage a wild bird, he said; once captured, you must first allow it the wider space of an aviary, and only gradually further imprison it in a cage. The need, among those trying to help gypsies, for all the virtues just stressed is obvious. (And incidentally, if you the reader, like me, find the actual analogy of caging the wild bird somewhat distasteful, it is worth asking yourself in passing whether you and I and others in animal-loving England do not have more concern for wild animals, for the state of safari parks, zoos and racing stables, and for pet cats, dogs or canaries, than we do for the well-being and living conditions of gypsy families.)

I myself wonder whether the particular freedom gypsies enjoy may not be akin to the freedom of those who do not know the voice of the Shepherd Christ, and would look upon any belonging to a church as a definite curtailment of liberty. Yet for me, it is a humbling experience to mix with people who have themselves grown from being travellers to settling, so that their sons and daughters could enjoy the benefits of education. However hard that initial sense of loss of freedom may have been, some of their children have come through from illiteracy at home to university education and then professional positions.

Jesus Christ moved on from the house of Israel to wider fields of differing belief and non-belief. It may be that those whom we meet in such fields today may shy from us as people who bind insupportable burdens. But we need to be going out all the time among those who are thus frightened, and we can only be persuasive in leading them to Christ, if we can exhibit in our own lives the sense of joy and freedom, of fellowship and love, which they will recognize as beyond anything they have yet experienced in the liberty they claim they possess.

In the past figures like St Paul have claimed loudly that they lived in a new freedom when they found or were found by Christ. I personally have met the same experience among those who have come to know him and hear his voice after years of living deaf to him. They use such words as 'new found freedom', 'liberation', 'coming from darkness to light' and so on. It is a real experience, and as shepherds, we must pray to be able to help others towards this experience.

For there are very many who thus far in their lives have never felt this. In one sense of the word, we who believe may feel that they are 'lost'. I do not of course mean outside salvation, but lost in that, from the believers' viewpoint, they do not see the one signpost which would lead them beyond where they now are.

Others are 'lost' in a different sense, and they need our compassion and ministry of healing. Love, caring, concern ... these words are easy to let slip from the tongue. The shepherd Christ turns us into shepherds of the lonely pensioner, the unvisited sick in hospital or home, the drug addict, the alcoholic, the despairing suicide, the crazy-mixed-up-kid. He asks us to seek out the over-successful and empty person, as well as the child or man born-to-fail. There is so much misery, so much pain. He himself came into it and relieved it physically, mentally and spiritually. Without him, or today without the Christian who is following in his steps, the misery and despair can turn the 'lost' against God and the very thought of his existence.

Finally, the Good Shepherd led his flock through suffering, abandonment and death itself, by giving up his life for his sheep. And he left behind with his disciples a message for anyone who would come after him: 'Let him deny himself and take up his cross and follow me.' (*Matt.* 16.24) This is tough for us to take, and so we have to sit down and ponder out the call, for in answering it we face growing into shepherds on the Christ-model; we face the task of going out to find the lost; and we face the final call which is inevitable for the shepherd, whatever particular form it may take in individual lives – Christ's blue-print for his kind of successful shepherding in John 12.32: 'I, when I am lifted up from the earth, will draw all men to myself.'

6

I AM THE BREAD OF LIFE

Despite all the variety of foodstuffs available to the modern housewife in Britain and for that matter in most of the Western world, an announcement of a further rise in the price of bread still has an emotive quality which gives it political importance and a lot of airing in streets, corner shops and supermarkets. Bread matters to people. If we think back to the Gospel scene at the end of Christ's retreat in the desert, we find the tempter suggesting that Jesus would have power to change stones into bread. Behind this lies not only the temptation of a very hungry young man to self-satisfaction in the shape of being able to produce something to calm the hollowness in his stomach, but also the power of food to govern the lives of human beings.

The reply of the hungry Christ, who was perhaps for the first time experiencing real hunger pains, recalled the past history of Israel and looked forward to words he would use in the future: It is not by bread alone that man lives, but by every word which proceeds from the mouth of God.

It is not very easy, nor is it very sensible, simply to tell a starving person that God is good or God will provide and to offer no food. Yes, how often in our ordinary way of living do we accept-by-ignoring the basic facts of the world of our time with its widespread misery and multiple deathroll following malnutrition. Those of us who were brought up in history lessons on the story of the beginnings of the French Revolution may be horrified or amused at Queen Marie-Antoinette's 'out-of-touch'

67

suggestion, be it true or apocryphal: 'If they haven't got bread, let them eat cake.' We are not so quick to realize that we are repeating such scenes simply by the way we continue to live in expectation of higher standards of pay and comfort.

A considerable amount of the teaching of Jesus Christ centres upon food as the foundation upon which he can build. For the great truth of Jesus Christ is that he is realistic, down to earth. Though his doctrine is leading all the time to the fullness of life which will only be found in the resurrection and life which he himself is, the here-and-now message is in terms that anyone can translate to his time, his place and his development. This point was to my mind put very beautifully in a recent church document:

> While he was on earth Christ revealed himself as the perfect communicator. Through his 'incarnation', he utterly identified himself with those who were to receive his communication and he gave his message not only in words but in the whole manner of his life. He spoke from within, that is to say, from out of the press of his people. He preached the divine message without fear or compromise. He adjusted to his people's way of talking and to their pattern of thought. And he spoke out of the predicament of their time.
>
> Communication is more than the expression of ideas and the indication of emotion. At its most profound level, it is the giving of self in love. Christ's communication was, in fact, spirit and life. In the institution of the Holy Eucharist, Christ gave us the most perfect, most intimate form of communion between God and man possible in this life, and, out of this, the deepest possible unity between men. Further, Christ communicated to us his life-giving Spirit, who brings all men together in unity (The Pastoral Instruction on the Means of Social Communication).

Jesus in that startling passage which comes in St John

Chapter 6 is out-spoken in his reflection on why the crowd has followed him, and he takes the opportunity to bring them forward from simply the material, substantial food which he has already provided to a beautiful and terrifying confrontation with his reality: 'I am the bread of life. Your fathers ate manna in the desert; and they are dead; he who eats this bread will live forever.'

In my thinking on the 'I AMs', the 'bread of life' is very closely linked to 'I am the vine', and also to 'resurrection and Life'. But in my understanding it goes on into the life-giving effect that my eating the bread of life will have on other people. I realize that there could be no better opportunity than here to enter into a discussion of Eucharist, but I am diffident to do so because I am not a theologian and the breadth and depth of the controversy which has been and still is in existence frightens me. Therefore, I will merely attempt to put one or two simple pastoral considerations for thinking and discussion. In these latter I hope you will refer both to the Gospel and to some of the many books available.

Discussion is most particularly necessary across the division of the Church, so that the ecumenical dimension can come alive. There is currently available, but not necessarily very much read, the *Agreed Statement on the Eucharist* by theologians of the Anglican and Roman Catholic Churches. There is the background to the emergence of the United Reformed Church; there is the whole rather sad but yet hopeful-for-the-future story of Anglican-Methodist talks. The material is here; the danger is that with so many strands of dialogue at a theological level, the ordinary man and woman in the pew may not grow at the same rate and even in the end not speak the same language, verbally or mentally.

To me it is a great help now, and was a jump forward in prayer and life when I realized that the primary presence of Christ in the world today is in people. Both his promise of indwelling and his assurance that where two or three are gathered in his name there he will be were from that time on in a new way real. Common belief in Jesus Christ and living in union with him in prayer is the staple diet of the Christian, cutting through all barriers of doctrinal difference at a level where coming together is possible. I have no doubt at all that there should be more effort concentrated on praying together. We can certainly study together as well, but the prayer is an aspect which is less controversial, more easily entered and also more binding. We need to grow together at all depths, mentally and spiritually. Where it is practical to be silent together in God's presence, allowing Jesus to fulfil his side of the promise and be there present, even without our understanding how, we do grow together. The same period may be used a little for praise and thanksgiving and even for meditative study of the Gospel. If you have not tried this, then the richness of the experience may as yet evade you, but if you ask anyone who has, then I think you will find that he will say it is a powerful way of paving the path to unity.

It could be said, of course, that there is danger in this. The danger is that we begin to experience the background of Eucharist in the prayer and praise, the gathering together, and the thanksgiving and joy which this creates within our community. And the logical development is towards real sharing of the Eucharist, which at the time of writing is still forbidden by the discipline of some of the major churches, including my own, the Roman Catholic Church.

However, one of the reasons for writing this section is to remind those who are likely to forget, and to say for the first time to those who have not yet heard: inter-communion is already going on in an increasing way. We may continue to pretend that it is not happening; theologians and church prescriptions at various levels may forbid it. But the truth of the matter is that because the people of countries throughout the world have their own attitude and background, the ruling is differently applied. This is especially noticeable – rule or no rule – among younger people, who find such a depth of common bond in sharing prayer that they flow naturally into the sharing of the bread of life without bothering with the niceties and to them irrelevant details of theological understanding. Put in other terms, an intuition of Eucharist as a *means to unity* grows in such people (and not only the young) to the detriment of the strongly held principle that shared Eucharist is a *sign of unity achieved*.

It is as though the life of Christ which comes through Baptism and Christian living feeds those who come together in his name, so that they are able to appreciate the depth of commitment to Christ in each other, to share the meaning of the real presence of Jesus Christ in the Eucharist, and so to come to share Communion without any misgiving, because this seems to fulfil the love of Christ.

Now I am not myself putting forward a position on the theology or the discipline, because as I have said I am not sufficiently schooled. But I cannot help saying that I pray day in and day out that common worship may be developed speedily, and that the Spirit of God will lead us all through what could be an endless maze of words and ideas into a clear acceptance of the purpose and desire of Christ. In the meantime, whether the churches agree or disagree, allow or forbid, it is only realistic to acknowledge the actual and almost certainly continued growth of inter-communion, going ahead of the law.

Those who agree that sharing is good, and so live it out, meet the tension and even the development of a 'nonsense' which emerges now in the sharing of churches and the sharing of tabernacles, especially where the priests of two different denominations hold the same theology of faith in the real presence. It may be that there could be fear of indifference or blurring of the essence of faith in the sacrifice and commemoration among the faithful who worship; but if we face the truth of the situation, the theological literacy at a scientific level of ordinary believers is not in practice far advanced.

I must leave it at this point ... in the air. My hope is that however woolly and possibly controversial the above paragraphs may be, they will lead to discussion and growth together.

'I am the bread of life' is not just narrowly eucharistic in the sense of the Lord's supper, the Mass. You see, as he himself says: It is not by bread alone that man lives, but by every word which proceeds from the mouth of God. And you and I who, through no merit of our own have been given the free gift of faith to live by, believe that Jesus is the eternal Word, spoken by the mouth of God. We speak of Holy Communion as Sacrament, but we are as much involved in sacrament when we are involved with the Word as he proclaimed himself, and as we are to proclaim him. There are no doubt technical differences of language and understanding, but both are life-giving, life-bearing. And I want now to draw out the way in which the word leads to bread and the bread to word and the word should lead to bread again.

You will recall the passage in John 6 where Jesus expounds the 'bread of life' theme. Do you remember as well that as a result of this forthright speaking some who till then had been his followers said that this was too much and that they would follow him no more? Jesus then directly challenged the close disciples: 'Do you want to go away too?' And out of this challenge comes Peter's reply: 'Lord, to whom shall we go? You have the words of eternal life; and we have believed and have come to know that you are the Holy One of God.' Here, the cycle is very complete: Jesus feeds the people and then when they follow, he makes it clear that words are necessary; the word-teaching will eventually become substantial at the Last Supper, but now the words are strong meat indeed so that only the 'mustard seed' faith of Peter reverts back to the Word, whom as yet he only hears imperfectly.

So it is through Jesus as Word that we gain life and

strength in believing: Jesus listened to in silence; fed upon in contemplation; read between the lines of scripture: all so as to reveal God 'through his Spirit in the inner man and that Christ may dwell in your hearts through faith'. There is a whole wealth of contemplation here, which is beyond our human imagining and which like the mustard seed can grow and grow, if we will give the seed the chance by allowing it darkness, silence, stillness. And, certainly in my personal experience, its growth leads directly towards Eucharist as the bread of life.

But the teaching of Jesus was a whole. He gave himself wholly, and I suppose at base this is the problem we face or run away from in our individual and collective lives, we who profess to be followers of Jesus Christ. Because he is life it is by 'tasting and seeing that the Lord is good' that we allow this life to nourish us and are in this way transformed. We cannot attempt anything here other than a hint, but I would like to follow through one aspect which to me is derived from here and is key, though I sometimes feel we Christians have lost that key.

If we are filled with Jesus Christ, or even begin to sit at his feet and listen, to me it seems inevitable that he challenges whole areas of our way of life. That is a superficial statement of something which should be obvious enough, but I put it here because I am concerned that we are diluting his message, speaking the harsh realities of his call indeed, but having spoken them, feeling satisfied that we have done enough. We are rather unprepared as we read Christ severely addressing 'the rich' to accept that he is addressing us. Pause a moment ... I mean pause ... and in the pause ask yourself the simple question ... Am I rich or poor?

Pause ... am I rich? ... Pause ... am I poor?
Pause ... What am I?

Obviously, riches and poverty are relative. The exercise which I have asked you to do, I want to ask you to do again a little later. Why? Because it is very easy to deceive ourselves. Recently I heard a tape of a doctor talking on the question of self-deception and this will illustrate what I am getting at. He said a man came to his surgery as a new patient. He explained he ran a public house. The doctor questioned him on his background, health, family, etc., to get necessary information, and then asked him if he drank at all. Not really, he replied, just a little social drinking. Pressing him, the doctor got the response that he never drank spirits. He felt he must probe further and the detail was this. What I do, said the publican, is to put a dozen pints under the bar when we open in the morning, and if I am offered a drink, I have one of the pints. I go on like that till they are finished. That's my lot. Then in the evening, I do the same thing, a dozen pints under the bar, I drink them until they are finished. This man, the doctor said, did not think he had any drink problem, though he got through twenty-four pints a day!

Is this kind of self-deception true of you and me in relation to our use of money and our accepted standard of living?

My point is that Jesus as the bread of life, if we get deep into listening to him, says loud and clear that we ... that is you and I ... must feed the hungry, clothe the naked and so on. Do we do this? If so, how much and, to put it bluntly and crudely, at what cost to ourselves?

Take this passage from one of the documents which came out of the Second Vatican Council called *The Church in the World of Today*.

God intended the earth and all it contains for the use of all men and peoples, so created goods should flow fairly to all, regulated by justice and accompanied by charity. Whatever forms property may take according to legitimate custom and changing circumstances, this universal destiny of earth's resources should always be borne in mind. In his use of them, man should regard his legitimate possessions not simply as his own but as common in the sense that they can benefit others as well as himself. But everybody has a right to a share of the earth's goods sufficient for himself and his family. So thought the Fathers and the Doctors of the Church, who taught men were obliged to help the poor, and that, not merely with what they did not need themselves. In fact he who is in extreme need has a right to supply this need from the riches of others. Since so many in the world suffer from hunger, the Council urges men and authorities to remember that saying of the Fathers: 'Feed a man who is dying from hunger – if you have not fed him you have killed him.' Each as far as he can must share and spend his wealth in coming to the assistance especially of these suffering individuals or peoples so that they may thereby be enabled to go on to self-help and self-development.

Strong meat! I wonder where I really stand on that? I sit in God's presence at prayer and I say to him: I suppose I am all right, Lord, because I am a priest and I don't really have much money; I give something to the poor and try to serve people; I do not have a car and I do not smoke. Then after a bit there is a little growing niggle which says (in the voice of God?): Yes son, you're all right until you think about three meals a day, and sometimes the odd snack too; you do not smoke, but what about your drinking habits? Just how much do you serve people ... count off the hours you spend on others and the hours you spend on you.

I took part in a three-day session of prayer with about forty others, priests, sisters and lay men and women of differing ages, background and status. We had periods of quiet, we shared prayer, one or two of us gave short talks to stimulate thought and prayer. It was very peaceful, very good, very deepening. But on the last morning each of three of us spoke about the Holy Spirit for a few minutes. I was rash enough to say more or less what has been written in the few preceding paragraphs. At once there was a rise in temperature. In every direction there was protest and disclaiming. There was every kind of reason given for possessions, even down to costly knick-knacks; they ranged from being reasonable to God's love of beauty, from leaving something for the children at death to real questioning of the demand Christ makes.

I instance this because we have grown to accept certain standards and indeed rising standards, in which we gradually include more and more. How many today think as an accepted condition of life in England that there should be a TV set, a car or even two, a summer holiday (possibly abroad), and cigarettes, a drink, and three lots of food a day? It is stupid for me to go through the list. The question is whether we can re-align our sights, re-adjust our perspectives. Because almost anyone who reads this in the Western world will be comparatively rich.

This is not easy to appreciate, except in deep thought, in contemplating Christ, and in trying to develop a sense of the wide, wide world. Let me give you an illustration from my own experience in the Caribbean, a couple of years ago. One day on the island of Dominica, where I was visiting families of those who had emigrated and now live in London, the local radio announced that the biggest banana shipping firm had cancelled all collection of bananas till further notice. Why? Because in England there was a strike by dockers. I have forgotten how much they were demanding extra per week; perhaps ten pounds, five hundred a year, extra. As I drove up into the mountainous interior of the island, men, women and children were carrying their crop of bananas down for collection to the roadside. They had not heard the news; their harvest would not be collected; their annual income, which probably would not total the extra demanded by the dockers, would rot until the dockers were satisfied.

This may not be a very good illustration, but it hit me because I knew I was living in the same way as the dockers, or miners or priests or civil servants, or teachers or publishers. My 'poverty' in Christ's service is richness to two-thirds of the world. But on coming back to England, I am at once taken into a society which is largely blind to the reality. I then have to ask myself whether it is possible to live and proclaim Christianity with truth, if we are spending money, energy, the world's resources – everything at a prodigal rate, and largely for our own comfort, our own development, our own often selfish, often unnecessary standard of living? Please pause . . . ask *yourself* this question too.

Are you prepared to face the issue that there probably is no other way to carry out the word of God in Christ than by accepting willingly and working all out towards a lowering of our standard of living, in order that we can share more fully with others? I realize this is a crude statement and economists may speak differently. All right, but they then must find a way for more even distribution, and our change of heart is still necessary.

In a sense, until we go without, we do not know how well we can get on without. The urgency of Christ's message is still with us. But here and now not only individuals but the Church and the churches have to take steps to implement the message. Christ, bread of life, feeds us physically and spiritually, without regard to himself. His 'follow me' is a real command; but for those of us who do not like to admit it is too hard, there is the alternative of editing to our taste. If we do this, we should perhaps call ourselves something other than Christian?

If Jesus feeds us with the bread of life, himself, then he says to you and me: Go and do the same. In all honesty, are we doing this? Is this the witness of ourselves, our churches and even our preaching today?

I find a direct connection between Jesus': 'I am the bread of life', and the last judgement story: 'When I was hungry you fed me.' But also, I see no way through to a widespread change of heart other than prolonged prayer, beyond meditation into contemplation, with a powerful call to the Holy Spirit. Pause a minute to consider this before you read any further.

Bend the stubborn heart and will
Melt the frozen, warm the chill,
Guide the steps that go astray.

7

I AM THE LIGHT OF
THE WORLD

I don't know Who – or what – put the question, I
don't know when it was put. I don't even remember
answering. But at some moment I did answer 'Yes' to
Someone – or Something – and from that hour I was
certain that existence is meaningful and that, therefore,
my life, in self-surrender, had a goal.

From that moment I have known what it means 'not
to look back', and 'to take no thought for the
morrow'.

Led by the Ariadne's thread of my answer through
the labyrinth of Life, I came to a time and place where
I realized that the Way leads to a triumph which is a
catastrophe, and to a catastrophe which is a triumph,
that the price for committing one's life would be re-
proach, and that the only elevation possible to man lies
in the depths of humiliation. After that, the word 'courage' lost its meaning, since nothing could be taken from
me.

As I continued along the Way, I learned, step by
step, word by word, that behind every saying in the
Gospels, stands *one* man and *one* man's experience.
Also behind the prayer that the cup might pass from
him and his promise to drink it. Also behind each of the
words from the Cross.

Dag Hammarskjöld wrote these words on Whit
Sunday 1961, and they help to throw into relief for us a
phrase which Jesus used more than once, according to
John's Gospel: I am the light of the world. To me, they

are useful at this point because they express so finely the mixture of light and dark, certainty and groping, which somehow characterize what has elsewhere been called 'dazzling darkness'. Let us reflect for a while on this mixture.

The second of the occasions when Jesus spoke of himself as light was at the moment of his cure of the man born blind. (*John 9*). This has always been one of the most precious stories in the whole of the Good News of Jesus Christ, because of its ring of humanity and truth, its realistic details, and its final call to follow. Jesus is always setting us down-to-earth examples. Though it is easy for us to wriggle and remain blind by finding soft interpretations of them, their challenge once squarely faced is highly demanding. Part of the reason for this wriggling is that, powerful as the human reason is, Christ has a way of leaping ahead of us in thought or action. In this particular case, the light he has given to the man who was blind and now sees is sight in the literal sense. It cannot be argued that the man cannot see, because he is standing there seeing. But the observers can produce various explanations. It can be said that it is a different man, that some imposter is having them on. Or it can be said that the whole thing is a trick, played perhaps by the Evil One . . . The one thing which is not so acceptable is the hard truth that God is behind it all, God in the person of '*one* man'.

So Christ takes those who see or hear of his action through the process of regaining sight physically and at the same time teaches the light of faith through the cured man. He could not have had a better medium to teach through than the man he chose, with his straight, clear acknowledgement of the truth and his determination to stick to his account, against all the cajoling and threatening of the learned men who intellectually knew so much more about these things than he did; and actually seemed so blinded, rather than enlightened, by what they knew.

The word which comes to my mind here, is the word

'experience'. It does not seem possible to 'teach belief'. This does not mean that belief is against reason; it does not mean that we are released from the human logic of using reason as far as we can in pursuit of belief, and in underpinning belief by every method we can find. But, when all is said and done, belief, faith, whatever you want to call it, is still beyond our unaided human grasp.

This is really worrying to some people, and it is to make the way easier and more 'arguable' that creeds and theological studies have been worked out and completed and used down the ages. Even the most deeply faith-filled of us still likes to have a word or system of words to fall back on or cling to, or even to fight against.

And yet, over and beyond this, is the still 'undefined' God, who is 'undefined' because he is not subject to our defining, he is not small enough to fit into the compass of our minds:

> O world invisible, we view thee,
> O world intangible, we touch thee,
> O world unknowable, we know thee,
> Inapprehensible, we clutch thee!
>
> Does the fish soar to find the ocean,
> The eagle plunge to find the air –
> That we ask of the stars in motion
> If they have rumour of thee there?
>
> Not where the wheeling systems darken,
> And our benumbed conceiving soars! –
> The drift of pinions, would we hearken,
> Beat at our own clay-shuttered doors.
>
> The angels keep their ancient places; –
> Turn but a stone and start a wing!
> 'Tis ye, 'tis your estrangèd faces,
> That miss the many-splendoured thing.

Francis Thompson may be outdated for some, but he

touches the 'intangible experience' of our God-contact in this poem, setting the limit to our knowledge and carrying us beyond into experience. It is the same kind of expression in different terms as that of the man born blind or of Dag Hammarskjöld. Each of us can only reach that point by being enlightened, and there is no telling how, when, where (or even if) that enlightenment will come.

It is one of those difficulties for our human reason that God does not seem to have given us a certain way other than the Way, which is Jesus Christ. And the experience or living of Jesus Christ comes differently to each of us, so that we can try to help each other in discovery, but we need each to be discovered. The reality is that strange mixture of light and dark, worldly and other-worldly which brings us from the first part of Francis Thompson's poem to the last verse:

> But when so sad thou canst not sadder
> Cry; and upon thy so sore loss
> Shall shine the traffic of Jacob's ladder
> Pitched betwixt Heaven and Charing Cross.

Christ leads the man born blind to the day by day living of belief: 'Do you believe in the Son of Man? ... You are looking at him; he is speaking to you.' The man said: 'Lord, I believe', and worshipped him.

Here is an immediate, down-to-earth challenge to us. We must face squarely the possibility that we (that is you and I) are, as we read and study this, sitting in the place of the Pharisees, and so are liable to the judgement Christ gave of them when they declared: We are not blind! (*John 9.40–41*)

This deserves careful, thoughtful consideration, in which we lay ourselves open to the revealing light, and do not shift our mental gaze from the shafts which may be penetrating the more murky corners of our well-fortified selves. Open a crack. Let the light in. Though you may be afraid of what you will come to know of yourself, look back to Dag Hammarskjöld and see how 'courage' loses itself in understanding . . . or is it enlightenment . . . or is it faith?

When one thinks of the birth of a human being, one sees him coming from the warm safe darkness of the womb into the insecure light of the world. From that time onwards, there is groping and fumbling; there is learning by touch and then by hearing and then by seeing; there is a gradual co-ordination of these senses without knowing how this happens . . . learning, learning, learning all the time. But this is not just for a few weeks or months at birth and after; it should be a lifetime of learning, a lifetime of seeing more clearly, a lifetime when we can either be enlightened by light or darkened by it. Such is our freedom. The same light can illumine or blind. Your personal concern is to ask yourself and your neighbourhood community whether Christ, the light of the world, has illumined you, or whether, thinking you can see in his light, you are in fact blinded blind . . . and so your leadership as a Christian, individual or collective, is blind leading the blind.

I expect each of you watches TV regularly or at least occasionally. Some of you may have appeared on the 'little box' yourselves. If you are a viewer only, I wonder if you have considered how 'naked' the person on the screen is? Naked in the sense of 'exposed'. When I first began to appear a little on TV, I was introduced to the very forthright head of the company. He looked sternly at me. He paused, then said: 'Yes, I suppose you will be all right. You have to be honest on TV. It's the politicians who let themselves down . . . it's their eyes. You can tell at once if they mean what they say.'

As regards Jesus Christ I would want to say, firstly, that Christ, the light of the world, does mean what he says. However much his 'followers' or his 'friends' or even his 'church' may at one time or another edit or conceal, overemphasize or underplay any part of his teaching, if you look Jesus Christ in the eye, if you sit and look and listen to what he says – then you will know that he does not lie but he enlightens. What is more, he does not cover up for you, but he wants you exposed along with him in the light, so that you may be a child of the light, and preach his word in the light.

Then I would go on to underline that if you claim to be a believer, you are already claiming to be 'enlightened'. This is not a 'proud' claim, but it is one which leaves you in an exposed position. You are immediately available for attack, question, demand for explanation, and refuge in despair. However slight your faith, you are stronger than the man of no faith; however slender your strands of conviction, you will be expected to support your conviction convincingly.

I do not think that the average Christian likes to think of himself as in the front line: it is too exposed a position.

Nevertheless, it is true, from the outside. 'You are a believer in Jesus Christ?' says the unbeliever. 'Right! Explain to me how . . .' 'Oh,' you say, 'I can't really do that. You see I'm only an ordinary person. I'm not qualified to explain it all to you.'

But what are you then? What is 'ordinary'? Do you follow someone you do not believe in? Can you explain to me at all what it means to you to be a Christian? Is this something which is real in your life? Are you at least prepared to say the kind of thing the man-born-blind said? For instance: 'I don't know if he is a sinner; I only know I was blind and now I see.'

I suppose one of the troubles with most ordinary Christians, who have been 'born in the faith', is that they have never come to the position where they could state with the straight humility of the man-born-blind: 'I was blind, but now I see.' There are a few who are prepared to say this, but only a few. Now, I do not want to put myself forward particularly, but I admit openly . . . I did not believe; I was blind: but I also say . . . 'But now I see.' Ask me to give you a definitive picture of what I see, and I must refuse, because I do not think 'Who I see' is definable. Therefore, I am in an exposed position. I 'experience' someone or something. Perhaps I cannot express this in intellectually respectable terms. But through my 'experience' I am prepared to say: 'I am very sorry. I cannot put this in language you are likely to accept. But I just "know that my redeemer lives".' If you then press me further, I can begin to do with you what I am trying to do here ... to look into Jesus Christ, to see what he meant of himself, when he exposed himself to mankind in his followers. He came to enlighten; by being a Christian I already to some extent claim enlightenment ... this whole book then is in a sense me exposing myself to the world, in the light of what I have learnt of Christ in my own life.

I do not for one minute make a claim to special knowledge; indeed I would say that I am very ordinary in my thoughts. And I hope this self-exposure is not just boring to others, but rather an encouragement to them to come out themselves into the daylight with their own experience, their own enlightenment. You see, Christ not only claimed that he is the light of the world. He also said according to Matthew: 'You are the light of the world. A city built on a hill-top cannot be hidden. No one lights a lamp to put it under a tub; they put it on the lamp-stand where it shines for everyone in the house. In the same way your light must shine in the sight of men, so that, seeing your good works, they may give the praise to your Father in heaven.' (Matt 5.15–16).

This seems a very clear message. Be quite simple and crude with yourself as you face your Christian reality! What light is shining from you? How bright is it? How attractive is it? In your personal knowledge, has the seeing of your good works made your neighbours give praise to your Father in heaven?

The suggestion I want to make is this. We are likely to go along quite happily, even in our discontent, without serious upheaval or re-adjustment of our way of living, unless we allow ourselves time to come a step back from the busy-ness of life and lay ourselves open to the searching light of Christ.

The light has a profound effect upon us, if we allow its penetration to go deep into our being. Somehow, we know much more clearly that we must say 'Yes', with all that that will mean in self-surrender to whatever the demand of discipleship maybe. If we remain shallow and shut up against the light, our reaction to anything the least radical which enters our minds will be: 'God cannot really be asking that of me! After all, I have my family to consider; What will my friends say? I'm not a fanatic! Jesus only wants our reasonable service.' – Yes, it all sounds so reasonable! But does it really link in with Jesus who

> did not cling to
> his equality with God
> but emptied himself
> to assume the condition of a slave,
> and became as men are;
> and being as all men are,
> he was humbler yet,
> even to accepting death,
> death on a cross.   (*Phil.* 2.6–8)

This deeper knowledge or enlightenment is not an airy-fairy idea. It irritates and urges us on to a way of life which is only satisfied by positive action. What do I mean by that? I mean if you take the passage of Matthew on the light of the world, it is preceded by the Beatitudes and it is followed by a long account of the new and higher demands of the standard of Jesus Christ. The culmination of this passage is: 'I say this to you: love your enemies and pray for those who persecute you.' He goes on to explain that loving those who love us is nothing ... anyone can do it, even the tax collectors (who seem to have a pretty low rating!).

But, be honest! When did you last go out of your way to help someone who hates you?

When I face statements of Jesus Christ like this, I am left wondering what we Christians are really up to? I mean this at what I suppose everyone now calls the 'grass roots'. Do *you* open your house to the poor? Think not only in broad terms of all the respectable palaces and presbyteries, vicarages and rectories up and down the country – many under-used and tidy and oh so nice! But think also of all the big houses, the medium houses and even the small houses which are just as respectable, just as private, just as un-open to the poor.

A beggar comes to the door; he smells and he staggers. The smell is a mixture of alcohol, sweat, stale clothes, urine, and footrot ... a beggar leaves the door, and I go off to watch the TV, and then to stretch in a warm bed, as the rain seeps through the sack which covers the beggar as he lies in a derelict house. Next day, I say my prayers, I join others in the Eucharist, I thank God for all his mercies to me –and the beggar coughs his way through the rain to another humiliating day which will probably end at another door, which again will be closed ... for after all, there is Social Security, a Welfare State, workers paid to look after problems!

But, come off it, Christian! However many welfare states there may be, the poor will be always with us, on our own doorstep (only we don't want them there!), unseen behind newspapers in broken-down hovels. And they will also be there all over the world, only we can ignore them too, be blind to them.

Alexander Solzhenitsyn in his Nobel speech said: 'Mankind can only be saved if all men are concerned about everything; if all the people of the East are not indifferent to what people are thinking in the West; if all the people of the West are not indifferent to what is happening in the East.'

It surely must be my concern that people are homeless ... but is it? It surely must be my concern that people are

87

hungry ... but is it? It surely must be my concern that people are alcoholic, drug addicts, born to fail ... but is it?

The light of Jesus Christ helps me to know him and myself and the world. He has established us here; he knows our being, not only from outside but from intimate sharing. He knows we shall go through life, feeling forward in faith, whether in self-confidence or self-doubt. He puts himself firmly there in the Way and in our hearts, by his Word and Sacrament. Elsewhere in addition to saying 'Follow me' he says 'Learn of me'. He knows the self-questioning, the uncertainty of man. Bonhoeffer wrote in June 1939:

> If only the doubts about my own course had been overcome. One's own searching into the depths of one's heart which is nevertheless unfathomable – 'He knows the secrets of the heart'. When the confusion of accusations and excuses, of desires and fears, makes everything within us so obscure, he sees quite clearly into all our secrets. And at the heart of them all he finds a name which he himself inscribed: Jesus Christ. So too one day we shall see quite clearly into the depths of the divine heart and there we shall then be able to read, no, to see, a name: Jesus Christ. So we would celebrate Sunday. One day we shall know and see what today we believe; one day we shall hold a service together in eternity.

> 'The beginning and the end, O Lord, are thine:
> The span between, life, was mine.
> I wandered in the darkness and did not discover myself;
> With thee, O Lord, is clarity, and light is thy house.'

The confusion and darkness, the lack of will to do those things we begin to glimpse as right, these are aspects of what it is to be human. It is at least a first step to be able and humble enough to admit confusion and groping. Then we will need deep prayer to get us on our feet and into action.

Humanly it does not seem within the realms of possibility that everyone could face the confused issue of their lives and come through with the strength of Bonhoeffer, Solzhenitsyn or Hammarskjöld. But the offer from God is there in Christ, as Paul writes to the Ephesians (3.20): 'Glory be to him whose power, working in us, can do infinitely more than we can ask or imagine: glory be to him from generation to generation in the Church and in Christ Jesus for ever and ever. Amen.'

8

I AM THE TRUTH

If St Paul was physically alive in the world today, and had set his mind on writing a letter to the English-speaking Christians, what particular passage from one of his letters do you think he might be encouraged to repeat? I was thinking about this in a silly, wandering kind of way, and I came up with a suggestion to him that it would be very suitable to refer them quite simply to what he had previously written to the Ephesians. Especially, I suggest, chapter 4.

I would like you to read this chapter before you go any further, and to see then whether you have drawn from it the message which I have drawn, and which I am going to open up in the following pages. First, please read this chapter . . . now.

The part I want to highlight is this:

In particular, I want to urge you in the name of the Lord, not to go on living the aimless kind of life that pagans live. Intellectually they are in the dark, and they are estranged from the life of God, without knowledge because they have shut their hearts to it. Their sense of right and wrong once dulled, they have abandoned themselves to sexuality and eagerly pursue a career of indecency of every kind. Now that is hardly the way you have learnt from Christ, unless you failed to hear him properly when you were taught what the truth is in Jesus. You must give up your old way of life; you must put aside your old self, which gets corrupted by following illusory desires. Your mind must be renewed by a spiritual revolution so that you can put on the new self that has been created in God's way, in the goodness and holiness of the truth. (*Eph. 4 17-24*).

For me, the initial problem is that I read this not with myself in view, but thinking – Ah, yes! That is what Christians need to be told. I do not say immediately ... Michael ... that's you he is getting at! Look at the way you are soaking up the general world attitude round about you! Get to it; sort yourself out!

What about you?

Christ proclaimed he was the truth and he proceeded to 'live' the truth. Unless you and I accept that he is the truth, that he taught the truth and that he expects us to follow the truth, we are each in our own way under the censure of Paul.

The hardest step is to admit, as you read this ... 'Yes Lord! That's me!' It is too easy to be the pharisee going to the temple to pray ... I am not as other men ... rather than the publican ... have mercy on me, a sinner.

The next hardest step is to realize that for me, yes ME, this means not merely a slight change of direction, a new emphasis here or there, but that my 'mind must be renewed by a spiritual revolution'.

Paul writes of 'an aimless kind of life'. Does that fit me? What today should be called an aimless life? If we look at Jesus Christ and believe he is the example of living which God gives us in human nature, then we must see that his life is aimed all the time along the one track: 'I have come to do your will, O Lord.' His close bond with the Father keeps the vision and direction straight, even when side turnings are offered. His picture of life lived truly is life lived wth a unity of purpose which at the same time takes in a big variety of interests, contacts, relationships, work, success and failure.

Now Paul's worry, seems to be that 'the old way of life' and 'the old self', get 'corrupted by following illusory desires'. This makes such a life aimless in his sense, because the aim is diverted from the straight path of truth. It may seem over idealistic and too simple to say that in so far as Christians today allow themselves to be over crowded by the affairs of the rat-race, money, bettering themselves and so on, they are in danger of being corrupted without realizing it. Aiming for this world is itself an aimless pastime unless its beginning, middle and end are closely linked to God, prayer and the resurrection.

This is a hard saying. Certainly. But a true one!

A phrase which is often used by the questioners in *What's My Line?* is this: 'Is there an end product to your work?' Well, we who are Christians cannot afford to be side-tracked into a merely humanist position of world development as our end product, exclusive of God-values and God-dimension. This is not a condemnation of the world, for Christ specifically left his followers in the world to bring it to fullness of development. The world is God's creation; Christians have often neglected it and found themselves rightly condemned by non-believers who were changing the face of the earth without God, while believers shunned contact. There is much for us to learn or be reminded of by others, but we must go further than they do if they are just humanists, for we must assert by our life that we believe the truth of the 'everywhereness' of God; that he is interested and active throughout his creation, that he cares for one and all. Good as the humanist ideal is, much as we should welcome good humanists and their work for the world, we must live now and in the future 'betwixt heaven and Charing Cross'. Nothing less for us can be the fullness of truth, however near it may come in idealism and expression.

I wonder if it is too steep an ascent for us to climb from this point to face Christ in proclaiming himself as truth by proclaiming himself and God as One. 'I and the Father are one', he says. It is too much for the Jews because it makes Jesus God. There is also the intellectual difficulty of one and more than one, humanity and Godhead. But I want to look at it here a moment, because it highlights also the unity and diversity of the created Universe. I put it as a personal problem, because I find Unity and Trinity a focal point of mystery from which radiates every other mystery, including all the apparent contradictions. And here I am led either to dismiss everything as incredible or to fall on my knees in adoration at the Incomprehensible.

Sadly enough, part of my time, and I gather from much discussion with others part of the time of many or most men and women, is taken up in refusing adoration of the Incomprehensible, and in insistence on intellectual satisfaction. With Thomas, I and the world assert: 'Unless I see the holes that the nails made in his hands and can put my finger into the holes they made, and unless I can put my hand into his side, I refuse to believe.'

Unfortunately for me in this mood, and for others similarly, I am in a position to learn by adoration of the Incomprehensible things not given to man to see or know by his own reasoning. And if I *know* this is true, nevertheless by a quirk of my nature, I still often opt for my own reason. I suspect I feel more secure in not being able to understand, and have a better excuse for not believing, if I am relying on myself – than in giving my ability to understand, accepting not understanding, and so believing.

And what, anyhow, is it that I claim to know or see if I adore and contemplate? Frankly, it is difficult to say other than to use the one word God. What I know doesn't go into words, but it makes me say to God, as it were – 'Yes! I see.' Perhaps the experience is not meant to be available for communication in words. Possibly it affects me, and because of it my life-style changes; my values adjust; there is something of a 'spiritual revolution'. This is the truth. It is not necessarily obvious to you.

Oddly, one of the attitudes which emerges from this experience is a greater tolerance of diversity and a new sense of the meaning of unity. How single is one? How uniform is unity? Paul says: 'If we live by the truth and in love, we shall grow in all ways into Christ, who is the head by whom the whole body is fitted and joined together, every joint adding its own strength, for each separate part to work according to its function. So the body grows until it has built itself up, in love.' (*Eph. 4 15–16*).

The unifying principle is God in Christ, One, Love. But how quickly our minds work on that reality and diversify again. How simple and straight is Jesus' word: I am the truth. (*John 14.6*). Simple yet profound as Faith should be, yet the simplicity immediately makes the human being, in the person of Pilate, need to quibble on the meaning of truth.

Now the unifying spirit is the Holy Spirit and he is involved in this peculiar business by which we know truth the world does not know:

'I shall ask the Father
and he will give you another Advocate
to be with you for ever,
that Spirit of truth
whom the world can never receive
since it neither sees nor knows him;
but you know him,
because he is with you, he is in you.'

(*John 14.16–17*)

We understand that what Christ said was and is true. What he promises he fulfils. And so we believe in the coming of the Holy Spirit, but we are not always so good at accepting that we know him, because he is with us. But this also is true. And therefore it is important that every Christian becomes increasingly aware of the power, presence and work of the Holy Spirit in himself and in others and in the Church.

Jesus found it very hard in his own life to persuade people of his reality and truth. I suppose each one of us would like it if he were immediately self-evidently true. He is tantalizingly elusive. Now he is here, now he is gone. He hides and reappears. For long periods of life he may seem to have gone away altogether. And this puts us in a tizzy, because it seems so odd that this sense of loss should come, if he really is true.

In these times, it is a very real help if we have (if I may put it that way) cultivated our acquaintance with the Holy Spirit, and have become aware of his secret working. For Christ promised:

> 'the Advocate, the Holy Spirit,
>   whom the Father will send in my name,
>   will teach you everything
>   and remind you of all I have said to you.'
>
> *(John 14.26).*

He is, as John Taylor has called him 'The Go-Between God'. I remember before I was ordained, I was given a little prayer in French which I have kept with me ever since to pray before preaching: O Holy Spirit, you change our stupidity into wisdom; I feel you between me and those who listen to me; speak with me, speak for me. What I say will effect nothing if you do not stand between.

It is as though man is an electric light bulb. Until the contact is made with the power, he remains dark; and at the contact he is immediately alight. And yet the light is not his own. Let me illustrate from a personal experience. I was slogging away at this piece of writing, and finding it exceedingly hard to get anything into words. Then a man came in to see me to talk about himself and his wife and family, his work and his soul. In the course of the conversation, he said he wanted to share with me a particular incident which had overwhelmed him since we last met. His story was this. Running a business which includes a system of hiring out instruments, he had a certain customer in one day when he was very busy. The customer paid arrears of rental amounting to thirty pounds or so.

Being in a hurry, my friend put the money on one side with some work he was doing, rather than ring up the till half a dozen times for the top figure of five pounds credit. Later that evening, the thought came to him that he could evade the tax man by simply not crediting the money, and he left it where it was. But later still, he was praying, as he does regularly every day. In the midst of his prayer, the thought of the money came to his mind and suddenly he experienced the sensation 'You cannot do this. I AM THE TRUTH. You can not pray to me and decieve me'. He got straight up, went down and paid the money into the till. Never, he said, in his many years of prayer life had he experienced anything so inexpressible in its truth.

The story is real, and it happened while I was writing this. So the timing is real. I am not suggesting that this is fantastic. I am simply saying this is the kind of thing which happens. It can be called chance, coincidence, anything you like.

But when it happens not infrequently, you may come with me to call it the work of the Spirit, who is promised to lead us into all truth.

Then with me you have to praise God and thank him.

And afterwards, rejoicing, you have to get on with very ordinary living!

Now I would suggest that the dilemma and the choice which we are all up against is the challenge Jesus put to the Jews:

'If you make my word your home
you will indeed be my disciples,
you will learn the truth
and the truth will make you free.'

The (somewhat over-stated!) reaction of the Jews was: 'We have never been slaves to anyone; what do you mean?' And the very simple and straightforward (but difficult) response of Jesus was:

'Everyone who commits sin is a slave.
 Now the slave's place in the house is not assured,
 but the son's place is assured.
 So if the Son makes you free,
 you will be free indeed.'

(John 8.31–36).

I believe Jesus when he said: 'I am the truth'. I therefore believe in this promise of his. I believe the Son makes me free. I believe therefore that I will be free indeed.

Do you believe . . .? That is worth stopping and pausing over . . .

As Christians, we believe Christ came to save us from sin and death. We believe he came to give us new life. But still, like the Scribes and Pharisees we tend to remain chained in so many ways, we are not free. Why, I wonder is this?

I sense that people are afraid – of the unknown, of the boundless; afraid that they really will be alone on their own. But this fear is not justified because Christ has promised that both he and the Spirit will be with us always even to the end of time. But the fear remains . . . supposing all this is just eyewash? Suppose he did not mean it that way? Suppose I've got the wrong end of the stick?

There are a thousand and one reasons we can produce for caution. I wonder if caution is one of the gifts of the Spirit?

It is clear in the development of a person like Paul that there remains a deep difference between freedom and licence. In unthinking or immature minds the two easily become identified. The Spirit will alway leads us into truth, even through darkness. But again and again I find myself reiterating that it is necessary to spend time silently with God in openness, because otherwise there is danger of spinning off into outer space rather than being free with the freedom of the children of God.

Notice, it is the freedom of the *children* of God. One of

97

the qualities of the child perhaps is the ability to ask questions and to go on asking. The child is not always satisfied, and in any case may only be able to grasp part of the explanation. So we too in our relation to God will always remain glimpsing his truth, and (I hope) left conscious of the infinite amount more that has still to be revealed. Hence, the sitting or kneeling openly, often almost terrified by the distance that seems to separate our understanding from the depth of God's purpose. The freedom is a dizzying experience because in God there are no bounds except his being, which itself is limitless.

How difficult it is for man to accept this distance, how easy it is to misinterpret the freedom. The freedom of the child is only a happy freedom and only a safe freedom in relation to the parent. If in seeking freedom the child escapes the care of the parent, freedom can soon turn to tears, can even end in accident or death. Jesus let little children come to him. In one sense they may have experienced him and his reality more deeply than did their parents. A child is quick to 'know' the kind, the gentle, the loving; quick to sense disinterest or sham.

For the growing person, it is very different, because development needs some separation from the parent, if the young man or woman is to become rightly independent. Often there is a period when communication is difficult, when thoughts, ideas and even ideals are areas of conflict between the two generations. There is every likelihood that a similar pattern may emerge in the relationship of the younger generation to God, and to the image of God held by parents and teachers. In this period, we all need patience and sensitivity to accept the way in which God's economy is leading us forward all the time, if we make proper use of it ... leading forward through withdrawal, questioning, the challenge of new visions in the new generation. Both older and younger are affected and both will be led to fuller and fuller truth if we are willing.

The experience of Jesus, the experience of prayer, the

experience of the Spirit – all these the individual and the group need to taste. But because we are different in so many ways, older and younger, deeper and shallower, more and less experienced in joy, suffering and so on … therefore the experience I try to recount may mean little or much to you according to your own situation. If you are far advanced, it may be 'old hat' to you; if you have scarcely begun, it may seem 'beyond' you. Yet, if you accept the possibility and indeed rightness of difference, you will be re-inforced by what you already know, or spurred on forward by some word or idea at present too deep for you.

If we take the figure of Jesus Christ and sit in his presence absorbing his statement: 'I am the truth', then at this moment I can only gain what I am ready to gain from my own disposition and degree of openness. But also, I can only gain what he through his Spirit wants me to learn at this time. When he reveals himself in his lifetime, it is not everyone who has ears to hear. His own true words can alienate as well as win. Where he wins, the growth of understanding even among his disciples is slow, and at times seems not to have begun at all. When he sends the Spirit at Pentecost to lead them into all truth, they are still not fully there, and Peter has to admit later: 'The truth I have now come to realize is that God does not have favourites, but that anybody of any nationality who fears God and does what is right is acceptable to him.' (*Acts 10.34–5*).

When we consider that Peter is still learning after Pentecost and after already having gone some way in the preaching of Jesus Christ, we must surely ourselves be ever ready to follow the example of Peter in learning.

Incidentally, this advance or jump in Peter's understanding underlines what I have been saying repeatedly about prayer. Note the very human and to me personally recognizable background to his prayer: 'Peter went to the housetop at about the sixth hour to pray. He felt hungry and was looking forward to his meal, but before it was ready he fell into a trance.' (*Acts 10.9–10*). And then the trance goes on with a background of Peter's hunger, for it is the vision of animals and the invitation to eat.

Perhaps one of the aspects of the truth which Jesus tries so hard to teach us in his own life and words, is that we come to truth by the Spirit and in prayer and living, but that the living is normally very ordinary. Prayer and what we learn can be stimulated by sleepiness or hunger, by joy or pain, by emptiness or a bursting gladness. We must understand the truth that we should go to pray as we are, not waiting for a suitable mood or good feeling; God is as capable of teaching us through despair as he is of teaching us through joy. All that is needed on our side is the totally trusting childlike attitude: Here I am Lord. Do to me as you will. You have the words of eternal life. You are the truth.

9

I AM GENTLE AND
HUMBLE IN HEART

There is a sense in which this is an extra! It could well be said that it does not come into the same category as the other 'I AMs'. True! So here is my justification.

If we are to look at Jesus Christ and learn of him by learning him himself, then we would be foolish to miss the one occasion in the whole of his message when he makes this definite and direct command to those who want to follow 'Learn from me, for I am gentle and humble of heart, and you will find rest for your souls. Yes, my yoke is easy and my burden light.' (*Matt 11.29–30*).

I suppose it was from this phrase that there grew up a whole series of insipid pictures and even hymns featuring 'Gentle Jesus, meek and mild'. These gave a totally wrong impression and have left a legacy, even to the film world, of a caricature of the poor man of Nazareth.

For one of the things which it would be very difficult to distil from a reading of the Gospel is a kind of weakling, milksop Christ. Yet I wonder whether this is not an image which persists in the back of the mind of many people? If I am right, then, of course I would have every sympathy with those who cut away from any form of religion which they thought to be founded by such a figure: I could not follow that kind of person either!

An interesting development away from this is the Italian film director Pasolini's *Gospel According to Matthew*. As an atheist, Pasolini was won to the person of Jesus Christ by reading the Matthew account, which itself is responsible for giving us this particular line of Christ's teaching. There have been mixed feelings about what resulted, but certainly the Christ personality is not weak. And it is this conclusion which fascinates me, because looking myself at Jesus, I am immensely struck by his power, the force of his being, the strength which underlies all that he does, even at the weakest moment in the garden, where his whole being revolts and yet he can still say: Not my will but yours be done.

You know, I am sure, the sort of person I have in mind when I use the phrase 'a gentle giant'. We can imagine, for instance, a man who is physically large and powerful, a rugger tough for example or a heavy-weight boxer. He is indeed tough; he is physically overwhelming; he has muscles like steel bands. Yet he is intensely gentle, and delicately sensitive; he perhaps weeps at the death of a friend. And at the same time, he is strong in his principles; he is honest and upright; he does not run away from the truth. Perhaps this sounds like some-one 'out of this world'; but there really are people like him.

If this sketch means anything to you, then you can come some way with me in how I think of Christ. I am not of course urging the physical dimension as such, that is only an illustration. Rather what stands out in Christ is the mixture of power and gentleness, strength and sensitivity; it is the warmth of true affection and love tempered by the commonsense reality of knowing the human being as human; it is the spiritual quality of seeing deep into the heart, while rightly judging and sifting the externals. There is a quality of silence in his listening which is a quality of humility in one who is 'Lord of all'; there is a sense of confidence in his presence, because he does not cause fear but trust; he is one in front of whom you can really be yourself, and know that he weighs you rightly, does not laugh at you or despise you, but somehow lifts you and gives you new heart. When you have begun to appreciate him, you know the apparent contradiction that he will never let you down, even when you seem to have been abandoned by the whole world and even him.

You trust him when he says: I will be there – even when his presence is not obvious. So he builds in you that mixture of faith and outgoing love which is so utterly demanding of human nature that it calls forth a whole way of life that is virtually foreign, or even an apparent madness, to the 'inexperienced'. So this gentle giant goes on ahead, yet is always present, brings human arrogance to humility by his example, and turns human despair and self-depreciation into true acceptance of self, with all faults taken into account.

This leads me on to underline that humility is one of the virtues which requires the greatest strength of character, because it is the one which is lowly, yet dignified, utterly undemanding *for* self, and therefore utterly demanding *of* self. In its quality, it comes in my thinking very close to Paul's description of love: 'Love is always patient and kind; it is never jealous; love is never boastful or conceited; it is never rude or selfish; it does not take offence, and is not resentful. Love takes no pleasure in other people's sins but delights in the truth; it is always ready to excuse, to trust, to hope and to endure whatever comes.

'Love does not come to an end.' (*1 Cor. 13.4–8*).

To be of any value an example should, I suppose, be a combination of challenge with feasibility. If too much is asked, there will be too much to dishearten; if not enough, no one will bother. Now, the main example we have is Jesus, but before we look fully at him, let us learn from three predecessors, who stand out among others as faithful in love through humility.

I would firstly pick Abraham (originally called Abram until God changed his name), who became strong through weakness, and who humbly accepted the way in which God led him out of a comparatively settled life, so giving up security, to venture in a new land. He is very real, because he goes through the difficulties of life, and is so very unselfish, particularly in relation to his nephew Lot, who really played his uncle along. When they returned from Egypt, both now rich in cattle and possessions, Abraham allowed Lot to choose the land he would have, and Lot chose the obviously richer portion of the plains and valley, leaving the comparatively barren hills to Abraham. The latter did not murmur. And when Lot made a continual mess of things, ending in the problems of Sodom and Gomorrah, it was Abraham who pleaded with God to save the cities. Then again, God seemed to have promised Abraham a future inheritance for his descendants, given him visions of the stars of heaven with which his descendants would compare ... and yet at seventy or eighty years old, he still had no children and was advised by his wife to sleep with a servant girl. Ten years more, and still no child, Abraham humbly continued in faith, and when another promise comes that Sarah his wife will conceive and bear him a son, she laughs outright at the suggestion, because she has passed the change of life. Then he does indeed father a son by her; and as he grows in happiness with the lad, he is told to go and sacrifice him ... and off he goes. So the tale unfolds ... read it through slowly, trying to mark the time lapse, the endless patience, Abraham's willingness to accept his wife's advice, his compassion for Lot, his obedience ... and sit quietly asking yourself what kind of man this was. I would say a man faithful in love, by living in humility.

The next figure is John the Baptist. Again, what a life and what an example, as he acts as a bridge for Jesus to walk across on his mission to the world. For us, who live in a bridge situation in the world of today, yet stretch out all the time for the solidity of the other bank, here is an example of faith and love, shaded by a humility which accepts totally 'there is another greater than I'. Put yourself in his position; we too are in a Church in transit, in a world emerging into an unknown future, which is more imaginable in the pages of science fiction than anywhere else.

Finally, at the threshold of the life of Jesus Christ, is the young woman whom all Christians accept under the title of Mother of God, whatever their subsequent attitude to her or devotion may be. Her faith shines forth in her acceptance, when she says 'Yes' to God's message of offered motherhood. Her patience emerges in the trials leading up to and following the birth, and continues in her silence and pondering at mysterious events. Her humility is clear as she is 'neglected' by her son, in her widowhood perhaps; she remains always at hand, not pushing her position, but accepting his busy-ness, his care for others, his triumph and his degradation, and still being there. How much of humility is faithfulness in being there, with difficult husbands or wives, with the revolt of teenagers, with the errors and mistakes of youth, with the trauma of middle life, perhaps with the abandonment of old age? All the Biblical examples are very real, even though we may say in our minds that God would never ask that of *us*. I wonder if Abraham thought that as he climbed the mountain with his son, or John as he lay in prison, or Mary as she took her child and fled into Egypt . . . surely Lord, this is not the way you would treat your servant, let alone your son! Or did they not question, but simply went on without flinching or wondering? I doubt that! I think it is much more likely, in the pattern unfolded in history, that God's demands remain at a high level in relation to human standards, perhaps because mankind really responds much better to challenge. It is when our natural idleness and self-indulgence take a hold that we are least effective, least growthful.

And so – Jesus Christ. I wonder if you have come across the amazing life of Charles de Foucauld? When he was 'caught by God', he spent a long time looking for the real Jesus Christ, and more and more he was drawn to the poverty, the silence, the humility and the forgottenness of the hidden life at Nazareth. For one who had earlier been so much in society, so successful in the world, this was a call away to the desert – a desert which blossomed for him both in the obscurity of Nazareth and the final desert of the Sahara. It blossomed in silence, hard work, poverty of living, failure, and ultimate betrayal by a friend, like in his Lord's life. Now, let me confess it – ever since I was myself caught by God in a lesser way, I have been fascinated by Nazareth and the hidden life of Jesus Christ. This fascination is odd, because when I was first caught, I looked at the solitary and the contemplative life in a hermit and monastic setting; but in a short while, I turned away from both. Why? Chicken-hearted, I think – seeing the glow of attraction, tasting that attraction in the experience of living with Carthusians and Trappists, and then coming out from that into the noise of work in central London.

The silence and the humility of this long, long preparation of Jesus Christ still fascinates me. Is it that I am just too weak to follow his lead? Or is it not for me? Might it be in the future? I ask these questions, and I wonder if you do? Because, you see, our life may change, and after a full activity, there often follows retirement, death of husband or wife, a new form of living. But even earlier, there is that choice which is ours at some period in life, and perhaps more than once.

More basically than this, I am convinced that the noisy world of today needs a whole series of injections of silence and contemplation, with the development of patterns of prayer in the midst of the world, as well as withdrawal from the world. We believe Christianity will survive and that there is reality in Christ's words: Fear not, little flock, for I have overcome the world. But in history, we find not only survival but growth, growth through change.

It is for us to discover new patterns; it is for us to pioneer again in ways which will lead man to God. But the example is still the example which it is so hard for each succeeding generation of Christians to accept . . . the work of Jesus himself is founded on humility, realistic living, poverty and prayer. It is all this that builds up his example.

I wonder whether the human nature of Christ sometimes longed to use his powers so that he could triumph in the worldly sense. I wonder how much it cost him humanly to accept failure when there was so much persuasive power about in his character. I wonder how he tussled and wrestled with himself as he had to allow each possible avenue to success to be blocked off, simply because he was doing his Father's will, in humility, and was not there to use methods of pride which would ultimately destroy rather than fulfil.

In saying this, it would be a wrong balance to suggest that Christ did nothing, just sat and contemplated. In fact, we understand he belonged to a working family. But he 'grew in wisdom and grace before God and man' in that situation. My emphasis on the withdrawn nature of Nazareth is to adjust the balance of the work of Christ in preaching, healing, and so on, because the very hard task in front of men and women today is to stop working, to stop thinking, to enter silence, to withdraw and to learn in humbling darkness that God is God. This must be done, not against the preaching of the Gospel, but in order that the Gospel may be preached. The key note is humility, following Christ's example, because the ineffectiveness of our preaching stems not from the Word, but from the emptiness of the heart which speaks the Word.

I put the emphasis on humility at this point because for many it is going to be a dying to much of their present way of life, an admission that they were going in the wrong direction, and a rising again through the hidden power of Christ.

It is awful to realize how much of God's work, done by Christians, is in reality done without these same Christians giving much time or openness to receiving daily the only power which really works, the power of the Spirit.

Will you do something for me now, please? I want you to sit down, if you are not already. To stop reading after the next couple of sentences. I want you now to take a deep breath and hold it until you cannot hold it any longer. NOW . . . a deep breath . . . and hold it . . . and hold it . . . and hold it . . . let it out!

I hope you are now conscious of breathing? Unless you have asthma or bronchitis or are used to doing deep breathing exercises, this may be the first time you have breathed *consciously* today? Was it? Well . . . whether we are aware of it or not, we are breathing day and night, night and day. We know that if and when we stop breathing we will be dead! Yet, at night we certainly are not conscious of the in and out of breathing; and the normal person would go potty if deliberately concentrating all the time on this process which comes so 'naturally' to us as to be forgotten.

Right! God, you see, is as ever present and as forgotten as our breathing process. But, if you could become used to holding your breath now and then during the day, and while deliberately doing so, turning your mind and heart and being to God . . . you would in time become deeply contemplative . . . but you would have to submit humbly to the discipline and the absurdity of holding your breath as you sat still. Why not try that or some similar technique, and so develop what Brother Lawrence of old called the Practice of the Presence of God?

For this practice, which could also be called waiting on God, our attitude needs to be a humble one. It is rather like an adult going back to nappies, with everything being done and given for him and to him, his only consciousness being the capacity to say with his will: 'do unto me according to your word'; and with this surrender, there coming to him the realization that this will lead, in a way not known, to greater engagement than before both with God and mankind.

Such an attitude presupposes the acceptance of God in expressing his being as 'I AM'. It presupposes that this is God's promise at all times and everywhere: I WILL BE THERE.

In the humility and gentleness of faith lit by love, go forward, then, into the future hopefully and undismayed, in the joy of hearing Jesus Christ silently: I WILL BE THERE.

10

I AM THE RESURRECTION AND THE LIFE

I was called in one day to a hospital just outside the boundaries of the parish where I work, because one of the Indian mothers was in the maternity ward, and there was great danger of her losing her child. This was all I knew, but as her last child is suffering from spinal bifida, this particular confinement meant more to her, perhaps, than any since her first.

In the hospital, I prayed with her and gave her the anointing of the sick, which Roman Catholics take as one of Christ's sacraments and use frequently in hospitals and other occasions of serious illness. She promised to continue praying, and I said I and the parish would do the same. The baby was born, and we had a joyful family baptism at our church.

Then, after some six months, I was sharing a Eucharist with a family and their neighbours one evening at their home; when it was over, they introduced me to a friend from another town. She said: 'Oh yes, I know you. You came to the maternity ward where I am a sister to bless an Indian woman in her difficult confinement. You know God worked a kind of miracle?' I said I did not. 'Well,' she said, 'you see the doctors had lost the child's heartbeat for about two weeks, and they decided the baby was dead in the womb. Then, after the Mother had been anointed, a healthy baby was born, and the doctors could not explain it.'

Now, events like that can be easily held up for question,

medical evidence and so on. But when they occur, and I find they are not infrequent, these happenings shake me up, make me realize my faithlessness and echo the words of Jesus Christ: 'Oh you of little faith! Why do you doubt?'

I use the story here because it is a kind of resurrection, and the deep and difficult pondering which we are about to enter demands faith, because it is not basically wholly susceptible to the proof we would so much like in the case of Jesus Christ. If we accept the parables written by the early followers as recalling the actual words and lessons of Jesus, then we realize that he understood that even resurrection would not convince. The parable I particularly refer to here is in Luke 16, the story of the rich man Dives and the poor man Lazarus. It is worth reading and considering at this point, before we enter into our own thinking on the resurrection, because the warning Abraham gives in the text to Dives we ourselves could well ponder: 'If they do not hear Moses and the prophets, neither will they be convinced if someone should rise from the dead.'

When we seek out the phrase: 'I am the resurrection and the life', we find it in St John's Gospel, chapter 11. It is part of the beautifully human story of Martha, Mary and their brother Lazarus, great friends of Jesus. Lazarus dies and Jesus meets Martha and faces her, in the depth of her grief, with a statement which must have demanded quite exceptional faith from her, given that she knows the closeness of Jesus and her brother, and knows also that her brother is now dead:

'I am the resurrection and the life; he who believes in me, though he die, yet shall he live, and whoever lives and believes in me shall never die. Do you believe this?'

It is clear from the subsequent writing-up of the incident that it remained somewhere in the memory of the disciples. But it seems obvious from their behaviour at the death of Christ and at his resurrection that the full significance of what his words and actions had been teaching was temporarily lost on minds and hearts overwhelmed with a mixture of fear, horror, loss, grief and even despair.

Yet, when in the Acts we come to the early story of Christ's followers, we find that it is the witness to the resurrection which is the centre and mainspring of their activity. I find this helpful to me personally, because as I look at the long years of history which lead from Christ through to our present time, I am aware of the way in which different periods, different people and different situations evoke different lights on the person and message of Jesus Christ.

Gerard Manley Hopkins in one of his poems refers to 'immortal diamond' and links it with the resurrection of Christ and himself (the 'I' here meaning you and me also):

> In a flash, at a trumpet crash,
> I am all at once what Christ is, since he was what I am, and
> This Jack, joke, poor potsherd, patch, matchwood, immortal diamond,
> Is immortal diamond.

To me, it is important that the flash of immortal diamond which lit up the lives of the apostles and disciples in the early Church was the resurrection. As we go through the 'I AMs', we turn the diamond this way and that. At each angle a new glittering realization of the person Jesus Christ catches fire and, if we are willing, both lights and warms us with its radiance. But finally we turn the immortal diamond and it dazzles us with the brilliance and mystery of both light and hidden depth which is contained in the phrase: 'I am the resurrection.'

The very notion 'resurrection' needs to be clarified before we discuss the implications. In one sense, it refers to what happened once with Jesus when he passed through death to the new, risen life ... a foretaste of the glorious future awaiting us in the completion of God's plan. This is the prime meaning, for it is from this aspect that the others derive. The second meaning appears when it is applied to Baptism, and we speak with the apostle of going down in the waters of baptism to death and rising again in the new life. And then there is a third meaning, which can happen, and happen more than once, in the life of each and any individual. This is the resurrection which comes to the individual, waking him or her to the surrounding world in an entirely new way; it is like a sudden break and leap forward in our personal evolution.

I'd like to pass very briefly over the question of baptism and resurrection, because there is no space for an adequate discussion of it here. At the same time, it is difficult to grasp in the widely and traditionally practised Christian infant baptism the jump to new life which is so much more clearly evident in the kind of conversion or resurrection which happens to Paul on the road to Damascus. The only thought I would want to note is the 'subjective' loss which the child in baptism suffers, though I realize that this is not to be set against the effect of the sacrament. Certainly baptism needs a lot of study, perhaps alongside rethinking the emphasis on Confirmation. In these days in which we live, with the development of wider education and educational systems which evoke questioning among pupils and students, the need for each and every young person to face the challenge and choice of a personal act of faith is paramount. To have been brought up in a 'died and risen' state from soon after birth through infant baptism led on naturally in earlier, simpler and less secular times to at least occasional practice and nominal adherence. Today's climate makes the transition that much more nominal and less practising; and leaves the pastoral problem of very large numbers who have been taken to the waters of baptism but in whom the waters of baptism have not fully ᵍ'taken'. I am not here wishing to enter theological argument, but simply to register the close scrutiny which may be necessary to adjust so that there may be every possible opportunity for this basic sacrament of death and resurrection to bring those who receive it alive in Christ.

While I am not referring to Paul's baptism when I speak of his conversion, we can see in this extraordinary happening a whole death and a whole resurrection. His way of life is to be a zealot for the Jews, persecuting the followers of Jesus Christ. Of a sudden, all this is changed, he enters the darkness of blindness which could symbolize death and entry into the tomb; and then he regains his sight in the new life of Christ, who is both dead and risen. G. K. Chesterton in his book *Orthodoxy* likens such an event to turning a somersault. One minute everything is normal and the right way up; next minute it is upside down. The persecuted Christ becomes the hero, the persecutor becomes the follower. And this is no gentle development through intellectual study and reasoned approach to a new position. It is a sudden awakening into a new world: or indeed into the same old world, but now turned upside down so that values are changed, attitudes are changed, the whole driving force and direction of life are changed. From this time forward, Paul is the apostle of the resurrection. The Risen Jesus has resurrected Paul by making him pass over into the new life of the Christian: 'Behold I make all things new' is a reality in Paul.

It is important to note, however, that this does not totally discount or discard the earlier life of Paul. Rather for him it is the fulfilling of the old covenant. Not one jot or tittle is changed, and yet the perspective is so different that all is new. And the newness has the effect of liberating him from the bonds of the law into the 'freedom of the children of God'.

Unfortunately the word 'conversion' can have shades of meaning which do not always leave a good taste in the mouth. But conversion/resurrection of the Pauline kind, though not necessarily so dramatic as his, can and does happen to people of every race and age. It does not always prove as deep and true as was Paul's; the test of time can be too much for the first fervour. But where there is true depth, the change admitted by the person and noted by friends and neighbours can be profound, and its repercussions on others startling.

Once again, Paul helps here, in summing up the effect of conversion/resurrection on himself in Galatians chapter 2: 'I have been crucified with Christ; it is no longer I who live but Christ who lives in me; and the life I now live in the flesh I live by faith in the Son of God, who loved me and gave himself for me.' Conversion can get a bad name for itself when it is unrealistic, and does not appear in the Pauline terms. By this I mean that the impression can be given that a person is converted and at once carried into a different mode of being, whereas Paul is clear, both here and elsewhere, that being crucified with Christ is an essential element from which the life of Christ flows.

Even when something extraordinary happens in the life of a man, reaching beyond what we might call 'ordinary conversion', the reality of living persists. In Paul the hardness and suffering is made clear: 'Always, wherever we may be, we carry with us in our body, the death of Jesus, so that the life of Jesus, too, may always be seen in our body. Indeed, while we are still alive, we are consigned to death every day, for the sake of Jesus, so that in our mortal flesh the life of Jesus, too, may be openly shown.' (2 Cor. 4.10).

I have been privileged to be close in my lifetime to a man, Padre Pio of Pietrelcina, of whom the same has been claimed as of Paul. He bore the stigmata, as far as was humanly ascertainable, for some fifty years. He would seem to have gone through a death/resurrection experience; he was said to have many different powers. But to my first-hand knowledge, his life was ordinary, painful, simple, obedient, restricted, down-to-earth. And in living this life he drew to himself, and so to Christ, hundreds of thousands of people from all over the world.

We will certainly not many, if any, of us be called to live a Pauline or a Padre Pio life. But each of us, if we are earnestly following Christ, have to recognize and follow the straight way and narrow gate . . . in order to live and to have Christ living in us, we have to die. There is a direct link with pruning and suffering in the vine. There is a constant return to this in Scripture. And so we can now look at Christ saying elsewhere: 'Truly truly, I say to you, unless a grain of wheat falls into the earth and dies, it remains alone; but if it dies it bears much fruit. He who loves his life loses it, and he who hates his life in this world will keep it for eternal life.' From this, startlingly highlighted, we can see our own ultimate death and resurrection. Few things are certain. It is quite certain we are going to die. We do not know when or where or how, but in the long run we are all going to die. And the forerunner of our death is the death of Christ – on the cross.

It is important that we make quite clear to ourselves that Christ really did die on the cross. It is important that we do not think there is a fake here, a cover-up. No! He went into and through death, whatever that exactly is: and it is impossible for us to experience what this means, we who have not yet been through death.

The way of Christ's death is the way of the person who goes through death conscious almost till the last moment. People die very differently; some become unconscious comparatively early on, some die suddenly from a heart attack. In the case of Christ it was what we might call a recognizable dying. He had to face the issue, because he was deliberately put to death. He was not sick; he was not unconscious. He simply faced the beating, the nailing, the hanging and the dying. He was clear in his own mind he was dying. He died comparatively slowly and in great physical pain; he was also in mental pain, because he had been deserted by his followers; those who kept near him at all handed down the story that he was conscious to the end.

So Jesus Christ went through the feelings, emotions, desolation, loneliness of dying which will be surrounding you and me when we go through a similar process of dying, be it in detail longer or shorter, more painful or less. He is saying not only: 'I will be there' but: 'I have been there before'. Further, he goes beyond all this and says: 'What is more, I am the very life after you die; you will be coming through me and to me; I am the passover in person. Do not fear.'

The dying of Jesus is worth our thinking about and turning to with the purpose of ourselves facing death as it comes, and remotely before it comes, rather than attempting to hide it from oneself. In his case, it was not just at the last moment that he thought about it. He faced death at an earlier stage: he told his followers that it was necessary he be lifted up like the fiery serpent in the desert; he told them too that he must set his face to Jerusalem, there to be given up, beaten and put to death by his fellow men. Against protest from his friends, he still insisted on setting his face for Jerusalem, which meant facing death.

I would like you then, at this point, to stop a minute and ask yourself about your attitude to death. Do not push it under any mental carpet; do not pretend it does not really affect you. Take it out, look at it, live with it for a while. Mix it with what I hope is a real sense of resurrection. Do not be surprised by death because it is what life is all about.

Over and over again, I tell people of what to me is the lovely story of a couple I became very fond of. They had been married in middle life and were very closely and devotedly united to each other. The husband had a bad heart and over a period suffered severe heart failure. They both faced this calmly and together, and I went sometimes to be with them to pray and say Mass or give Communion. Eventually, he was in hospital for the last time, in desperate pain and dying, but fully conscious. The doctors said they were giving him an injection to ease him. His reply was: 'I want to go. I want to be with God! I'm sorry, love, I love you very much, but I want to go to God.' His wife stayed all night by his bed-side, and told me later they had a peaceful, quietly talking night, mingled with prayer and silence. Early in the morning he died, and we knelt and prayed again by his body.

Since that time, and hers is not by any means a unique case, his wife has lived on alone in the physical world, but very much alive to Christ's words: 'He who believes in me will never die.' I give this example, because her sense of the living presence of the risen Christ and of her husband's share in the resurrection has been the radiating force in her day to day life, and has proved a source of strength and hope for other people.

I wish we could all begin to learn to live our lives in the hope of the resurrection more like this. But the lesson we have to learn is Christ's lesson of accepting the cross, the suffering, the humiliation, and just the plain, ordinariness of dull grey living. If we do this day by day, then we prepare ourselves for death and resurrection, and live in God's presence, touched by his love. Sadly enough, we can profess to be dedicated to his service and working in his love, but pray hard not to die; we state our belief in eternal peace, joy, happiness, and yet in so many words and gestures say: But please keep me here in the toil and pain and sorrow of the world ... anything, rather than that I should die and be at peace! How strange we are!

Strange – yes! It is a very human attitude, however, because we hate to lose those we love – and we mostly hate to go out into the unknown. This is part of what I have tried to put in thinking of Jesus as the Way and the Door. ... It is a need to grow in faith and trust, as we ourselves go along, go through, are taken up ... in faith.

If we go along in faith, not knowing what tomorrow will bring, but trusting completely in him, then this same going along, this same process is the way we will die. For, learning daily more and more to live totally in Christ by learning daily to say 'yes' to life, we gradually give ourselves to him as a couple do in their marriage vows, only extended even further – for better, for worse, for richer, for poorer, in sickness and in health, to love and to cherish in dying and rising again.

The natural fear will continue to be there, but it will be balanced, and even over-ridden by this sense of union with him, and trust – this complete confidence – this real joy that we experience here and now in the growth of down-to-earth spiritual living.

To anyone who has not had this experience, it is hard to put across that this is not just pious talk in a sentimental strain, with little reality in the plain man's life. The only way I know of beginning to bridge such a credibility gap is in comparison with the human relationship of knowing and loving. The atmosphere or climate of prayer which envelops the individual is the atmosphere of loving and knowing that you are loved which grows in the prayer-relationship with God in Jesus Christ. If you know and love a human being and this love is returned, then you experience give-and-take, knowing and being known, loving and being loved.

Unfortunately, as human beings, if we have not experienced human love, we can pooh-pooh the idea; or we can say it is not for us; or we can retreat into an attitude that we are unlovable. It is, in my view, essential to break through such a barrier on the human level – and I speak now from working as best I can in and among people for over thirty years before and after ordination. It is normally possible, though sometimes extremely tough going, to break down the human barrier. It is only really possible with a strong mixture of interest, care, patience, regular contact, humility and love. And the process is very much one of dying and living again, or else of rising from the dead. It can be a true kind of resurrection, but it involves two people in the overcoming of fear, the opening of confidence, the development of knowledge and sharing – the beginning and growth of loving.

Without going into detail, I can think of one particular relationship in my own life where a complete brokenness of person which involved violence, theft, blackmail and other problems over a period of twelve or thirteen years eventually came through into marriage and a totally new life in a new country. Or another, where an utterly 'un-lovable' character, who has done a lot to try to destroy others and not infrequently attacked me, sometimes makes me want to end all contact in despair. Yet here, at the same time, I am driven endlessly to my knees, I'm kept alert to my own shortcomings in an unpleasantly direct way as I lose patience and courage and find love very hard. And, all in all the situation is not worse than at the beginning, and may even be better ... occasionally there are even signs, distant and glimmering, of new life.

I know that without having known love personally, both human and divine, I would have given up long ago. But to have experienced the radiant joy of waking up in the morning and knowing love is so mind-and-heart-blowing that I cannot help wanting to share it ... especially with anyone who up to now cannot conceive the possibility.

So, in the relationship with Christ-God, you grow to wake in the morning and live through the day with a sense of him; he is about, he is present. There is a sense of excitement at the very unknownness of the day ahead, because God speaks in the world and says: I will be there. You don't know what is going to happen, you don't even know what 'I will be there' will be like in reality. But somehow, in pain or joy, in worry or anxiety he will be about; and because he will be there, everything will be differently light and dark; there will be a little extra buoyancy, because you are in love.

You know what I mean? Or do you find it hard to believe? I can only say, if humanly you have been in love and lived on in love, it is like that . . . only not quite like that . . . and more so!

Part of love is trust. You now live in a trust relationship with Jesus. Worry and doubt are death, trust is the risen life, and so part of the trust is a growing inner acceptance of the words: 'I am the resurrection and the life' as applying now, in death, and afterwards. It is therefore more possible to face Jesus' question to Martha: 'Do you believe this' with a 'Yes, Lord' . . . which basically and truly means . . . 'Yes, Lord, I trust you.'

This faith-trust in Jesus Christ is vitally important in our own life. It is equally important in our translation of Christ to others. We can only help them to believe in him to the depth that we believe in him ourselves. This is one reason why so many are in such a confusion – they do not in truth believe deeply; they are not prepared to live by naked faith; they hark back to reassurance . . . when God only promises forward: I will be there.

Now the ultimate belief in him is the belief, and eventually the act, of dying in him. There is no greater demand upon faith in an individual than dying in Christ when the moment comes. And it is for that test that we need to be prepared by living the dying-in-Christ day by day by day.

How can anyone do that? Try now . . . and at other times, just to sit and hold the sense of death and resurrection. This is not to think about it, but to hold the sense . . . to hold yourself in God, in a moment, in timeless reality of Christ dead and risen again. Then, if your mind needs something, realize the problem the disciples had in recognizing Jesus in the resurrection. If we try to 'picture', we too may get the wrong idea. Mystery remains, a mystery of faith, in which, in silence, we have already experienced the joy of loving and being loved. Gently, we can allow an extension of that awareness to 'knowing' that the final resurrection-life with and in Christ will be infinitely beyond that present earthly experience.

This ties in very closely with the kind of death and

resurrection in prayer life. Often as we go about, we are consciously living our lives, we are making the running, we are carving out a niche, making decisions, having everything depend upon us. So in prayer ... it is I who use words, I think about God, by my activity I create a prayer-condition. But in reality, in growth, it is only when the 'I' gives over and dies to this notion of my own importance in keeping the relationship going that I can rise into the tranquillity of Christ working in me. This is a revolution, or a hand-over, which is very hard for those who have long been trained to do all the work. Suddenly, like a Pauline conversion, I accept that God is working in me, doing it all. I now feel that my constant activity is simply getting in his way, because I am imposing on myself my ideas of God, rather than opening myself to his reality, to be conveyed in his way, at his time ... and therefore more profoundly, more comprehensively and more sensitively than any effort of mine could ever achieve.

Death and fear of the unknown can be seen in our apparent loss of direction, the disappearance of signposts, of ways which previously we took to be methods of advancing. Before, perhaps, if we spent the time 'saying our prayers', we really felt we had been saying something to God. Now it may be that there does not seem to be anything to say. We dry up, in speech and thought. We are reduced to silence, and unless we see this and seize upon it as not death but a new way of life, dying in speech, rising in silence, we will fight to retain speech in what can be an agony like gears being forced wrongly.

Our mind images also fail. Unless we realize that we can be liberated beyond our limited thought pattern, we struggle to understand; thinking we are being truly human and rational, we chain ourselves to the confines of the mind, instead of going so far as we can, and then allowing ourselves to be seized by God. As eventually we have to surrender in death in order to live, so here and now we have to surrender to the higher order of God's working in us. Very simply we have to say to him: 'I do not understand, but teach me.' And he does so, in such a way that we know and still do not understand, because he is infinitely un-understandable to our finite minds.

It is not that we now never talk again to him. Indeed we praise him more loudly and more often. It is not that the wonderful gift of intellect which he has given us is abandoned for ever. Indeed we find greater heights and depths previously untouched. But God says in his silence – 'Listen! Wonderful as your mind is, I am too great for it; clear as your sight is, I dazzle it; big as your heart is, I overwhelm it. Therefore, if you love me as I love you, listen in silence, learn in darkness. It is through living that I taught you; my way was poverty, humility and suffering. It is along the way you meet me, it is in Gethsemane you sweat it out with me, it is on the Cross you die with me.

Boris Pasternak captures something of Christ's own passover through suffering and death to new life:
Unresisting he renounced
Like borrowed things
Omnipotence and the power to work miracles
Now he was mortal like ourselves.

He gazed into the black abyss
Empty without beginning or end.
Sweating blood, he prayed to his Father,
That this cup of death should pass him by.

Having tamed his agony with prayer
He went out through the garden gate
There, overcome by drowsiness,
The disciples lay slumped in the grass.

The book of life has reached the page
Which is the most precious of all holy things.
What has been written must be fulfilled,
Let it be so. Amen.

You see the passage of the centuries is like a parable
And catches fire on its way.
In the name of its terrible majesty
I shall go freely, through torment, down to the
grave.

And on the third day I shall rise again.
Like rafts down a river, like a convoy of barges,
The centuries will float to me out of the darkness.
And I shall judge them.

If we have the courage for this kind of death, the light
of rising filters through all the other parts of our life, our
thought, our seeing, our loving. His silence in us leaps out
in praise; his dark-light in us flashes new insights as we
move through real situations in life; his felt-absence as
well as his felt-love open understanding in us of the variety of feelings, emotion and response which different
events call from us in relation to him and others . . . for he
will always be there!

But, of course, one of the important elements, and this
was perhaps especially true for the disciples after the resurrection is recognition. 'I will be there.' But you and I, in
faith, in silence and in love must learn to recognize that
he is there.

So we come once more to the central problem of accepting Christ as Resurrection and Life. We cannot an-
ticipate our death, or even our day by day dying. We can
only live it; I cannot tell what it is like till I get there. I
would always so much like to look over the wall, to tear
down the veil, to have a preview of what passing over will
be like. But the nearest I can come is in faith, in dying
today and rising today, in preparation for my ultimate
death and resurrection. In this it is imperative that we
keep before us always the life and death of him whom we
follow. For we go ahead into the unknown, led out by
him; and yet we need to keep very close in our consciousness the sense that he himself on the cross went
through the agony of sense-loss which utters: 'My God,

My God, why hast thou forsaken me' and passes to the supreme trust of: 'Into your hands I commend my spirit.' We too, then, go forward utterly dependent upon the God in whom we cannot even feel belief, trusting in the Lord whom we deeply trust and still doubt; learning that 'love is repaid by love alone' even when we feel drained of everything; knowing that dying we live—

and now and every day accepting as true his promise:

I WILL BE THERE.